# TOUCHDOWN GENIUS

## THE UNPRECEDENTED FOOTBALL PLAYBOOK TO UNLEASH YOUR OFFENSE AND MAXIMIZE YOUR COACHING CAPABILITY

### POWER 5 EDITION — VOLUME 1

## XOS PLAYMAKING

COMPRISED OF 25 COLLEGE FOOTBALL
CHAMPIONSHIP SCORING PLAYS

# CONTENTS

# +35 YARD SCORING RUNS

# +35 YARD SCORING PASSES

## HIGH RED ZONE SCORING RUNS

## HIGH RED ZONE SCORING PASSES

# GLOSSARY

| ABBREVIATION | DEFINITION |
|---|---|
| #s | Numbers |
| $ | Sam Linebacker or Nickel Back |
| BOT. | Bottom |
| BOUND. | Boundary |
| BC | Boundary Corner |
| BS | Back Side |
| BSG | Back Side Guard |
| BST | Back Side Tackle |
| C | Center |
| DE | Defensive End |
| DIV. | Divide |
| DB | Defensive Back |
| DBP | Dropback Pass |
| DL | Defensive Line |
| EMLOS | End Man on the Line of Scrimmage |
| EOL | End of Line |

| ABBREVIATION | DEFINITION |
|---|---|
| FC | Field Corner |
| FS | Free Safety |
| FSL | Formation to the Sideline |
| HEELS TO TOES | Player is positioned in front of another player, aligning his heels with the behind players' toes |
| I.S. | Inside |
| I.S./O.S. | Wing player's inside foot aligned with the outside foot of the offensive tackle |
| IZ | Inside Zone |
| LOS | Line of Scrimmage |
| MDM | Most Dangerous Man |
| MOF | Middle of the Field |
| MOFC | Middle of the Field Closed |
| MOFO | Middle of the Field Open |
| OG | Offensive Guard |
| OL | Offensive Line |
| O.S. | Outside |
| OT | Offensive Tackle |
| OTB | Over the Ball |
| OZ | Outside Zone |

| ABBREVIATION | DEFINITION |
|---|---|
| PAP | Play Action Pass |
| PS | Play Side |
| PSG | Play Said Guard |
| PST | Play Side Tackle |
| QB | Quarterback |
| RB | Running Back |
| RPO | Run Pass Option |
| SAC | S-Across Motion |
| SL | Sideline |
| SS | Strong Safety |
| TE | Tight End |
| TIB | Tailback Into Boundary Motion |
| TIF | Tailback Into Field Motion |
| TOES TO HEELS | Player is positioned behind another player, aligning his toes with the front players' heels |
| WR | Wide Receiver |
| XAC | X-Across Motion |
| YD(S) | Yard(s) |

# KEY

| SYMBOL | DESCRIPTION | DENOTATION |
|---|---|---|
|  | 1 Grey Dash Through Line | Play Fake |
|  | 2 Grey Dashes Through Line | Ball Exchange Via Handoff or Toss |
|  | Circle with Vertical Line | Pre-Snap Motion Player Resets Before Snap of Ball |
|  | Dashed Line | Option Route/Assignment |
|  | Grey "T" Shape | Run Blocking Assignment |
|  | Grey Upside Down "T" Shape | Man Pass Protection |
|  | Long Square Angle Blocking Assignment | Pulling Blocker |
|  | Short Square Angle Blocking Assignment | Slide (Zone) Pass Protection |
|  | Thick, Black Line | Route or Path of Potential Ball Carrier |
|  | Thin, Grey Line | Blocking Assignment |
|  | Triangle Enclosing Defender | Read Defender |
|  | Wavy Line | Pre-Snap Motion |

# 1

# INTRODUCTION

---

*"Every choice, every decision, everything we do every day, we want to be a champion."*

— COACH NICK SABAN

---

I WILL NEVER FORGET that exhilarating feeling of scoring my first touchdown.

Raindrops soaked our offensive coordinator's play sheet as he ushered in the call from the sideline: Trips Right Fake X-Jet Z-9. We broke the huddle, and I jogged out to my usual Z-receiver position: top of the numbers, feet staggered with my inside foot up, slight bend in the knees, 80% weight on my front foot, ready to explode off the ball. The cornerback defending me stared at me through the rain as I mentally rehearsed my assignment.

"Ready!"

The X receiver began his jet motion.

"Set...Hut!"

I fired off the ball as the quarterback and X receiver performed the fake jet sweep. In order to sell the fake, my job was to break down and shoot my hands at the corner, displaying intentions to block him and seal the edge for the jet sweep. Once he committed to stopping the run, I was to release downfield into my 9 pattern, a number from our team-specific route tree representing a vertical route straight down the field.

The play action fooled the defense as intended, leaving me wide open. I looked back as I ran downfield and saw a beautiful spiral headed my way. The ball landed safely in my hands. With nothing but green grass in front of me, I sprinted the remaining length of the field, capping off a 60-yard touchdown.

Ever since that memorable moment, I've been enamored with the sensation of reaching the end zone. I was only 11 years old at the time, but I knew that I wanted to replicate that euphoria as often as possible – as a player and as a coach. The purpose of this book is to provide you with the necessary tools to produce that immense gratification for yourself and your teammates by manufacturing explosive, touchdown-scoring plays as you operate a championship offense – no matter the level of football in which you participate.

Whether you are a first-time youth football coach, an aspiring big-time ball coach just entering the profession, or even an established veteran looking to expand your knowledge, this book will provide both basic and advanced football knowledge and strategies to assist you in creating an offensive game plan that will terrorize any defense that dares to line up against you.

Maybe you are not a coach, but a current player. You may even be a once-a-week intramural or flag football league player. Your team does fine, but you lack conviction in your concepts and repeatedly fall just shy of that championship t-shirt. Or perhaps your plays feature the correct concepts, but you are missing the schematic familiarity of how to set them up and call them at the opportune time. This book will give you the advantage that you need to separate yourself from your rivals. Use the philosophies from this book to call the perfect play in the perfect situation and provide your team with the best opportunity to be successful as you repeatedly find your way into the end zone.

If you do not fall into one of the two aforementioned categories, perchance you are like I was: a dedicated college football fan. You spend the second Tuesday in January through the first Saturday in September wishing it were football season, then September through December watching the games, tailgating, competing in fantasy leagues, and publicizing your hot takes on any social media platform you can get your hands on. This book will give you an insider's analysis on what drives a championship offense. Impress your associates and discredit the online casuals with the analytical tools you will gain from indulging in this never-before-published content. You will be able to wow them with your expertise in college football schematics. If that superiority does not align with your personal motivations, then you will at least be able to take pride in the fact that you understand how your favorite college offenses operate as they dissect defenses with ease.

How can you not be romantic about football? Growing up, I waited every year (not-so) patiently for football season to begin. When it finally did arrive, I spent every Saturday with my eyes glued to the television, beginning my weekend at 7:00 a.m. to tune in to ESPN's timeless spectacle, College GameDay. I would then watch every subsequent game that both live cable television and DVR would allow. The only time I recall taking a break is when I would leave for a few hours in the afternoon to play in my own football games. Even at night, football occupied my thoughts. I dreamed of being on those football fields, hearing the roar of tens of thousands of crazed fans, leading my team to victory, and yes, scoring touchdowns.

But I'm not just a football fan anymore, and those dreams weren't just dreams. I have been fortunate enough to turn them into a reality.

I know what it takes to be successful at the highest levels of football. While my two Pacific Youth Football League Super Bowl trophies remain on display, I was not satisfied stopping there. After contributing to an undefeated, conference championship offense in high school that averaged well over 40 points per game, I was blessed to receive an opportunity to play college ball. In college, I immediately started at wide receiver, finishing every season with the team's highest in-game, player performance grade and eventually earning back-to-back all-conference honors. Now, it is my privilege to coach Division I College Football.

Given my offensive background, it is fair to assume that I make my living coaching on that side of the ball. However, my current role is as a defensive analyst. It is my responsibility to study and dissect opposing offenses until I understand and can thoroughly explain the "why" and "how" behind their successes. My job on the defensive side of the ball affords me a unique perspective. I know what frustrates defensive schemes and keeps defensive coordinators up at night. After meticulously studying the contents of this playbook, you will have an excellent idea of how to do so yourself.

This is not just a playbook of 25 random plays that I feel will convert your team into a champion. You could find that anywhere, created by anyone. Each of these plays was designed by professional coaches and expertly executed for a touchdown in an actual college football championship game. They have proven to be successful against the best defenses in college football.

Perceiving that it would simply be impossible to compile all the championship-worthy concepts and analysis into just one book, this unparalleled work is not intended to be a one hitter quitter. This is the first in a four-book series crafted for players, coaches, and fans who want to master the game of football. Each book in the series will dive further into the specific offensive and defensive concepts that we will discuss throughout this book, as well as introduce new touchdown-scoring schemes from other championship games. This is Volume 1 of the Power 5 Edition, which means that we will be looking at plays from championship games involving two teams from the five FBS Power 5 conferences. All 25 of them have scored touchdowns in either College Football Playoff National Championships, or SEC, BIG 10, BIG XII, PAC 12, and ACC Conference Championships. In other words, these plays were used by the best coaches in the league to score against the best defenses in the league. You will learn the names of these plays, the fundamental concepts that make them work, the perfect times to call them, and even potential adjustments that will tailor each play to your specific team and level of football.

The plays featured in this book have been divided into four categories: +35 yard touchdown runs, +35 yard touchdown passes, high red zone (between 15 and 25 yards out) runs, and high red zone passes. Therefore, each of the plays presented in this playbook were touchdowns resulting from explosive plays. Understanding that we cannot realistically expect to score on explosive plays alone, Volume 2 of the Power 5 Edition will feature only low red zone (from 15 yards and in) touchdown-scoring plays. Following the production of the Power 5 Edition, a Group of 5 Edition will be released, consistent with the 2-volume format of this current edition. In those 2 books, we will analyze touchdown-scoring plays from the conference championship games of the five FBS Group of 5 conferences: AAC, C-USA, MAC, MWC, and Sun Belt. The emphasis of this series is to demonstrate that the best way to operate a championship offense is by studying and doing what championship offenses do.

Not only will we study plays that are proven to score against the best defenses, but we will also describe in detail *why* they work. We will dissect and analyze each concept from their most basic foundations to their most sophisticated technicalities.

I fully understand that youth football players and coaches do not require nearly the same amount of schematic information as college and even high school football players and coaches. You have the freedom to pick and choose which material you will implement to benefit yourself and your team. If you are a coach, the more that you know, the better you will be able to instruct your kids. However, players are not obligated to possess the same knowledge as their coaches, so be careful about oversharing if all it will cause is confusion. Not all the info in this book is intended to be disseminated to your players. But, learning how the most successful coaches in the industry design and call plays will help you craft your own playbook and consistently place your players in winning situations.

In addition to offensive strategies, you will also gain defensive knowledge by reading this book. We will consistently walk through various, key defensive concepts ran by the opposing teams in these championship games. This defensive mindfulness will explain why these plays were successful against specific defensive schemes and will also provide insight as to how we can adjust our concepts to attack other defenses as well.

No other book like this exists on the market. Sure, some social media pages post screen recordings of specific plays from the most recent football weekend, but they merely mention the concepts used without analyzing them. That format does not help anybody who is trying to learn, only those who already know.

There are basic, youth and flag football playbooks out there, but they are created by authors who fail to explain why their plays work or give concrete evidence of their in-game success. Others out there are simply outdated, offering formations and plays that are no longer used in modern offenses.

Those books are not all bad, per se. They contain serviceable material, but they hardly scratch the surface. On the other hand, the book you are currently holding contains all the information you need to command a championship offensive game plan now. Each play has been battle-tested and proven in a live-action, high-stakes championship game within the last 5 years. The game of football has changed, and we must adapt to it if we wish to rise to the top.

As offenses have and will continue to become progressively more intricate, having an efficient, high-powered offense is no longer a luxury when it comes to winning championships at any level in today's game – it is a necessity. Fortunately for you, you are receiving unprecedented access to the very keys to success that drive the efficient, high-powered, championship offenses of today.

As you can see, this book compiles a ton of wide-spread and difficult-to-find football expertise. Legitimate, in-depth football knowledge encompassed in an organized fashion is challenging to lay hold of. Even if you are fortunate enough to find it, no one else is compiling that knowledge into an easy-access source that compares to the breadth and depth of the Touchdown Genius series. Rather than scour the internet, grasping at bits of information, and trying to piece it all together yourself, save your preciously limited time and shift your focus to the critical contents of this book. All the leg work has been done for you so that you may grow exponentially more than the average football fan, player, and even coach – in exponentially less time.

Football is my passion. It has always been at the center of my life, and I refuse to let my experience and knowledge go to waste. I know first-hand that coaching is an extremely difficult profession to break into, and an even more difficult profession to excel in. Unfortunately, there are few coaches willing to share their gift to help younger coaches. It is my calling as a successful player and coach to pass my knowledge on to football's next generation.

I have experienced the rigorous routine required to win football games at all levels, even youth football. I know the feeling of spending many hours in a week creating a game plan and then speculating all night before the game whether it will be successful. I know the frustration of searching for credible football information scattered across the internet, wishing it were all in one place, and never truly finding the answer to my apprehension. But I also know the instant gratification of scoring six points on a brilliantly designed and brilliantly executed play, and then doing it again – and again. I know the pride of staying one step ahead of the defense, winning close games, and bringing home championship hardware.

That pride and gratification can be yours.

# 2

# TERMINOLOGY

---

*"It's not the will to win that matters...everyone has that; it's the will to prepare to win that matters."*

— COACH PAUL "BEAR" BRYANT

---

BEFORE DIVING deep into the analysis of these 25 championship plays, it is critical that we harmonize our individual football dialects. Clear, consistent communication is vital to the success of a championship football program. If the language that we use as coaches does not translate to the players in a comprehensive manner, the negative repercussions will be manifest on game day.

There is an infinite number of terms utilized throughout the sport to refer to various elements of the game. What one offensive line coach refers to as an outside zone blocking scheme, another one may refer to as stretch. This chapter will clearly standardize the vernacular that will be used throughout the Touchdown Genius series – and any other XOS Playmaking-published book for that matter. We will discuss the following foundational principles of football anatomy: positional lettering, common formations, offensive personnel, formation strength, backfield strength, formation tags, pre-snap motions, and numbering threats.

## POSITIONAL LETTERING:

If you are a regular viewer of ESPN's Manningcast, an alternate broadcast of Monday Night Football, you may be familiar with Peyton Manning's demonstration of how NFL play calls are relayed from the quarterback to the rest of the offense.

"Alright, let's go boys..." he began, "...Let's go explode Gun Rub Right Flip Zebra, Scat Left, Y Drag, X hook, F Trail, Can, 52 Sprint Draw Easy on two, on two, ready break."

Did you get all that? It's a mouthful, but it is actually much simpler than it sounds.

On offense, each of the six skill positions is designated a letter of the alphabet. The most common examples are X and

Z as wide receivers, and Y as a tight end. Manning's play call is simply stating each skill positional letter, followed by their assignment. There is no regulation guide that dictates which letters correspond to which positions on the field; it is unique to every offense. I have played in offenses that refer to the strong side slot receiver as the S. Other offenses that I have been a part of label the same position with the letter F. No matter the letter, the key is to standardize the positional labels for your offense. The system that will be followed throughout this series is as follows.

Q – Quarterback

T – First running back (tailback)

X – Farthest outside wide receiver to the left (excludes tight ends and running backs)

Z – Farthest outside wide receiver to the right (excludes tight ends and running backs)

S – First slot receiver (11 and 20 personnel slot receiver)

V – Second slot receiver (00 and 10 personnel only)

Y – First tight end; down tight end and/or strong side tight end in multiple tight end sets

U – Second tight end; up tight end and/or weak side tight end in multiple tight end sets

H – Third tight end in multiple tight end sets

F – Second running back in multiple back sets, weak side back or back closest to the football (fullback)

B – Third running back in multiple back sets

OT – Extra offensive lineman (6 offensive linemen sets only)

## COMMON FORMATIONS:

Each of the aforementioned positional letters will appear in analyses throughout the series. We will now examine how they will be presented in some common formations that we will encounter. Beginning the breakdown segment of each play in this playbook, you will find the formation label. It will look like this.

**FORMATION: GS TREY UP FSL**

This example comes from the first play that we will study in the chapter, +35 *Yard Scoring Runs*. Let's break down each component of this formation. It is comprised of three parts: backfield strength, base formation, and formation tag. The first segment, GS, indicates the strength of the backfield, gun strong.

The second aspect, the base formation, is Trey Up. "Trey" illustrates a 3x1 formation with the most inside threat to the three-receiver side attached to the core and on the line of scrimmage. This is most commonly portrayed as a tight end aligned in the down position (3-point stance, on the line of scrimmage, next to the offensive tackle). However, "Up" signifies that in this variation of Trey, the tight end is in the up position (2-point stance, off the line of scrimmage, still next to the offensive tackle). Since the tight end, being the most inside threat to the three-receiver side, is still attached to the core in his up position, we call this formation Trey Up.

*Juxtaposition of Trey and Trey Up. Notice the difference in alignment among the Y and the Z.*

The third and final component of this formation is the formation tag, FSL – formation to the sideline. Formation tags suggest an alteration to the base formation (please see the *Formation Tags* section in this chapter for an in-depth explanation of various formations tags, including FSL). There will not always be a tag attached to the end of every formation; many will be two-component formations consisting only of backfield strength and base formation. Therefore, our formation naming protocol will always be backfield strength first, followed by the base formation, and capped off with a formation tag, if applicable.

Below is the depiction of our example formation, GS Trey Up FSL. The running back is aligned to the strength of the formation, GS. The skill players' positioning indicates a Trey Up base formation. And the formation is set to the near sideline, FSL.

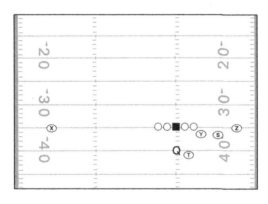

*GS TREY UP FSL*

Following are additional illustrations of common 2x2 and 3x1 base formations.

## DEUCE

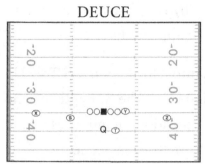

> 1 attached, down TE and 1 flexed WR to one side
> 2 flexed WRs to the other side
> 1 back in the backfield

## DEUCE UP

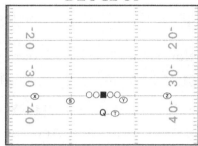

> 1 attached, up TE and 1 flexed WR to one side
> 2 flexed WRs to the other side
> 1 back in the backfield

*2x2 Formations*

## DOUBLES

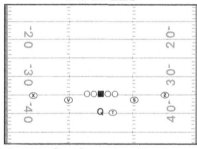

> 2 WRs flexed on either side of the formation
> 1 back in the backfield

## ACE

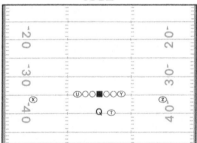

> 1 TE attached and 1 WR flexed on either side of the formation
> 1 back in the backfield

*2x2 Formations*

## TRIPS

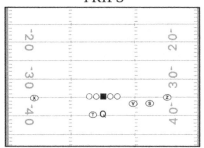

- ➤ 3 flexed WRs to one side of the formation; 1 flexed WR to the other side
- ➤ 1 strong on the line of scrimmage
- ➤ 1 back in the backfield

## TRIPS BUNCH

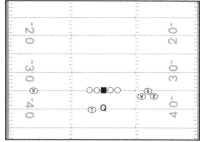

- ➤ 3 flexed WRs to one side of the formation, bunched together; 1 flexed WR to the other
- ➤ 2 strong on the line of scrimmage
- ➤ 1 back in the backfield

*3x1 Formations*

## TREY FLEX

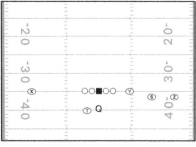

- ➤ 3 flexed WRs to one side of the formation; 1 flexed WR to the other side
- ➤ 3 strong on the line of scrimmage (usually a TE)
- ➤ 1 back in the backfield

## TREY WING

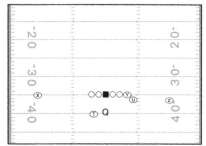

- ➤ 1 attached, down TE, 1 attached, up TE (wing), and 1 flexed WR to one side; 1 flexed WR to the other side
- ➤ 1 back in the backfield

*3x1 Formations*

## OFFENSIVE PERSONNEL:

Offensive personnel is used to refer to the various skill position players that are on the field at any given moment. It is presented as a 2-digit number. The first number represents the number of running backs in the formation, and the second number represents the number of tight ends. Since there are five available skill positions (not including the quarterback), simply subtract the sum of the 2-digit number from five to get the number of receivers.

The most common personnel groupings are:

10 Personnel: 1 RB, 0 TEs, 4 WRs

11 Personnel: 1 RB, 1 TE, 3 WRs

12 Personnel: 1 RB, 2 TEs, 2 WRs

20 Personnel: 2 RBs, 0 TEs, 3 WRs

21 Personnel: 2 RBs, 1 TE, 2 WRs

Below are some of our previously seen formations, now labeled with their respective personnel groupings.

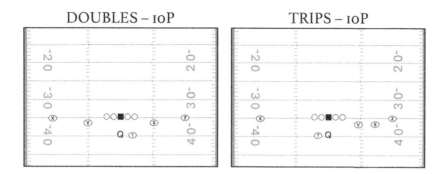

*10 Personnel Formations*

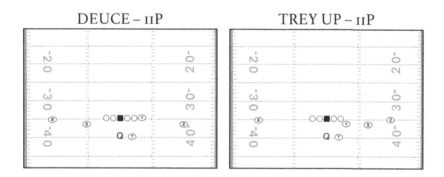

*11 Personnel Formations*

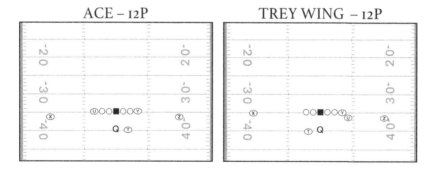

*12 Personnel Formations*

It is important to note that on-field personnel does not have to dictate out of which formations we can and cannot operate. We have to play our best eleven players. Say our tight end is one of our best players and offers significant value in the pass game. Our passing concepts should not be limited to what we can run out of traditional 11 personnel sets. We can easily line up in usual 10 personnel formations, like Doubles and Trips, with our 11 personnel by simply flexing the tight end out in a receiver position.

Having the versatility to do so will cause significant problems for the defense. Many defensive coordinators base their play call menu on offensive personnel so that they can match it with the correct defensive package. Operating out of differing-personnel formations with the same personnel package limits the defense's ability to substitute players and match what we are trying to do. This will lead to an increase in mismatches which we will capitalize on for explosive touchdowns.

Here are the same formations we just assessed, but with adjusted personnel groupings.

## DOUBLES – 12P

## TRIPS – 11P
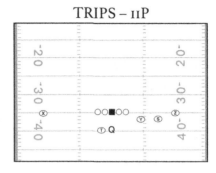

## DEUCE – 10P

## TREY UP – 10P
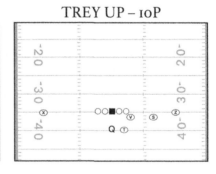

## ACE – 11P
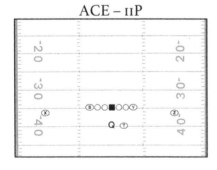

## TREY WING – 11P

## FORMATION STRENGTH:

The formation strength draws an imaginary vertical line through the center, splitting the offense in half. One side of the formation is declared the strong side, and the other, the weak side. For example, if we are aligned in Trips right, then the strength of the formation is to the right, and the weak side is to the left. This is because we have 3 receivers on the right side of the formation, and only one on the left.

However, declaring formation strength is not always as simple as identifying which side contains more players. Due to the variety of complex formations in the game, we must adhere to a specified protocol in order to accurately define the formation strength.

The order of operations is as follows.

1. Run strength
2. Pass strength
3. Field/boundary
4. Quarterback's throwing arm

Run Strength

A defense that is weak against the run stands no chance at winning. Likewise, an offense that fails to establish a solid run game is worthless. Even in today's throw-heavy style of football, games are won and lost by the big boys up front.

Their ability to consistently gash their opponents on the ground creates opportunity for explosive plays through the air – but it all starts with the run game. For this reason, formation strength begins with examining the run strength.

A formation has a run strength when there is either a down TE or an extra offensive lineman attached to the core and on the line of scrimmage. Run strength formations guarantee the offense at least 6 blockers in the run game that are already on the line, ready to fire off the ball and demolish any box defenders.

| DEUCE | TRIPS CLOSED |
|---|---|
| 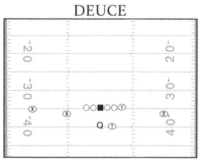 | 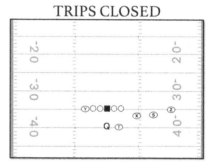 |
| ➤ TE to the right, attached to core, on LOS, denotes run strength to the right | ➤ TE to the left, attached to core, on LOS, denotes run strength to the left |
| ➤ Formation Strength = Strong Right | ➤ Formation Strength = Strong Left |

*Run Strength Formations*

## Pass Strength

If a formation does not have a down tight end or an extra offensive lineman, then it has no run strength. If there is no run strength, or the run strength is balanced, we then consider the next most immediate threat to the defense, which is the pass threat. The pass strength of a formation is the side of the formation that has the most vertical threats. A vertical threat is an offensive player either flexed outside of the core, or attached to the core and on the line of scrimmage. Backfield threats are not vertical threats.

| TRIPS | DEUCE UP |
|---|---|

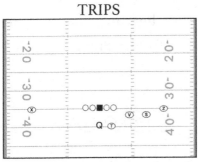 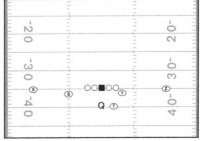

➤3 vertical threats to the right and 1 vertical threat to the left denotes pass strength to the right
➤T is not a vertical threat from the backfield
➤Formation Strength = Strong Right

➤2 vertical threats to the left and 1 vertical threat to the right denotes pass strength to the left
➤Y is not a vertical threat, he is aligned in the backfield
➤Formation Strength = Strong Left

*Pass Strength Formations*

## Field/Boundary

When a formation is balanced, meaning it has the same number of threats on each side of the formation (excluding backfield threats), then it has no pass strength, and we must declare the strength of formation based on field and boundary. Examining our imaginary vertical line through the center, the wide side is the field, and the narrow side is the boundary. So, if the ball is on the offense's left hash, then the field is to the offense's right, and the boundary is to the offense's left.

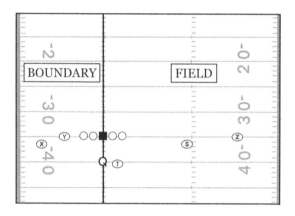

*Field/Boundary*

The strength of balanced formations will always be set to the field because that is that side that offers the offense the most space – the next immediate threat.

## ACE

## DOUBLES INVERT

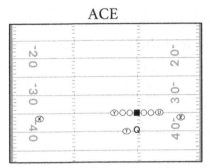
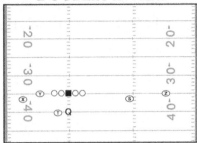

➢No run strength since down TEs are
  balanced
➢No pass strength since vertical
  threats are balanced
➢Field is to the left
➢Formation Strength = Strong  Left

➢2 flexed vertical threats on either
  side denotes no run or pass strength
➢Field is to the right
➢Formation Strength = Strong  Right

*Field/Boundary Strength Formations*

## Quarterback's Throwing Arm

In most cases, the previous 3 formation strength indicators will suffice. However, we may find ourselves in a situation where there is no run strength, the formation is perfectly balanced, and the ball is exactly in the middle of the field. In this rare situation, the strength of the formation is determined by the throwing arm of the quarterback. Following our next immediate threat model, the side of the quarterback's throwing arm indicates the strength of the formation because that is the side to which offenses are more likely to run quick game and boot action throws.

## ACE

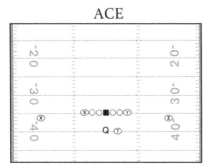

## DOUBLES

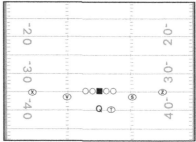

➢ No run strength since down TEs are balanced
➢ No pass strength since vertical threats are balanced
➢ Assume right-handed quarterback
➢ Formation Strength = Strong Right

➢ 2 flexed vertical threats on either side denotes no run or pass strength
➢ Assume left-handed quarterback
➢ Formation Strength = Strong Left

*QB Throwing Arm Strength Formations*

## BACKFIELD STRENGTH:

Understanding the strength of the backfield is an excellent tool we can use to create holes in our opponent's defense. Similar to the manner in which a defensive coordinator will base his play calls on offensive personnel, many defenses have pre-snap checks based on the alignment of the back(s) in the backfield. These checks generally adjust the alignment of the linebackers to reflect whether the back is aligned to the strong side or weak side.

As clarified in the *Common Formations* section, each formation name in this book will begin by labeling the strength of the backfield. The backfield strength informs the running back where to line up pre-snap. Since we will only be dealing with single-back formations in this book, we will stick to just breaking down single-back alignments (Volume 2 of the Power 5 Edition features many 2-back looks).

The running back's single-back formation alignments are home, gun strong, gun weak, and pistol.

## HOME

➤Quarterback under center
➤T aligned directly behind him

## GUN STRONG

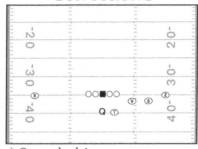

➤Quarterback in gun
➤T aligned to formation strength

## GUN WEAK

➤Quarterback in gun
➤T aligned away from formation strength

## PISTOL

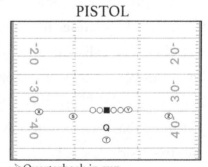

➤Quarterback in gun
➤T aligned directly behind him

FORMATION TAGS:

Formation tags are added to the end of our base formations to suggest specific modifications. These alterations are methodically designed to place the offense in an advantageous position prior to the snap of the ball. In this playbook, we will analyze four of the most common formation tags: invert, reduced, closed, and formation to the sideline (FSL).

## Invert

Inverted sets are ones in which a formation's usual threats aligned on or off the line of scrimmage are inverted, meaning the usual man on is now off and the usual man off is now on. A typical Doubles formation consists of the outside receiver lined up on the ball, and the inside – or slot – receiver off the ball. Doubles Invert, therefore, implies that on at least one side of the formation, the outside and inside receivers have now inverted their alignments. The outside receiver is now off the ball and the insider receiver is on. Inverted sets are often utilized if the inside receiver is running a vertical route. His formation-tagged alignment gives him that extra step he may need to take the top off of the defense.

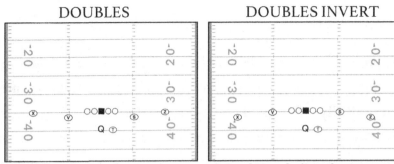

## DOUBLES

> X and Z on the line of scrimmage; S and V off

## DOUBLES INVERT

> S and V on the line of scrimmage; X and Z off
> Note: Both sides do not need to be inverted, just one inverted side will denote Doubles Invert

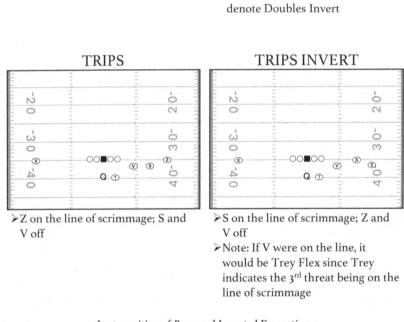

## TRIPS

> Z on the line of scrimmage; S and V off

## TRIPS INVERT

> S on the line of scrimmage; Z and V off
> Note: If V were on the line, it would be Trey Flex since Trey indicates the 3rd threat being on the line of scrimmage

*Juxtaposition of Base and Inverted Formations*

## Reduced

Reduced sets are easily recognized by the abnormally condensed spacing between offensive players. Rather than spacing themselves out evenly across the width of the field, the position players to at least one of the side of the formation are reduced down, leaving plenty of open field outside of the formation.

Offenses condense themselves to reduced sets in order to also condense the defense. By compressing the defense, we arrange two pre-snap advantages for our offense: mitigate the effort required to attack the edge of the defense, and enhance the probability of screening defensive backs in the pass game.

There is no universal distance between the end of the offensive line and the most outside receiver that dictates whether a formation is reduced. That technicality is for you to decide based on the capabilities of your offense. Just know this, the more you condense your formation, the better your chances are of finding space along the edge.

DEUCE

DEUCE REDUCED

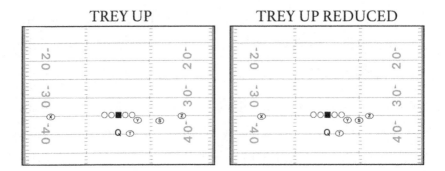

*Juxtaposition of Base and Reduced Formations*

## Closed

A closed set is one in which one side of the formation's most outside threat is a down tight end. This formation tag offers us a couple different advantages depending on which coverage the defense is in.

When defenses play zone, they seldom match personnel. So, we could potentially have a corner as the nearest pass defender on our tight end – a mismatch for the defense. In man coverage, defenses will match personnel. To avoid the TE/CB mismatch, the corner to the closed side of the formation will travel to the open side and man up on one of the receivers. This creates an advantage for us in the run game because the defense loses its edge defender in the run fit to the closed side. The most outside run fit defender will now be a safety. If we can seal the box defenders inside and get our back 1-on-1 with the edge safety, there is a great chance we find the end zone on an explosive run.

In single-back sets, all closed tags will apply to 3x1 formations.

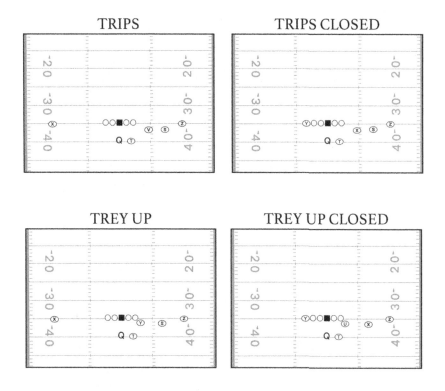

*Juxtaposition of Base and Closed Formations*

## Formation to the Sideline (FSL)

This term is also commonly referred to as FIB, formation into the boundary. Whichever wording may be familiar to you, the concept remains the same. An FSL tag indicates that the side of the formation with more offensive threats is set to the boundary instead of to the field. Backfield threats are not considered when identifying FSL formations.

When dealing with 3x1 formations, FSL identification is easy; the 3-receiver side being set to the boundary constitutes the formation as FSL. However, 2x2 formations complicate the process a little. In these instances, we consider the side with more flexed, vertical threats to be the formation side that will dictate whether or not the formation has an FSL tag. If a 2x2 formation is perfectly balanced with the same number of flexed vertical threats on either side of the ball, then it is not deemed FSL.

As with the other formation tags that we've broken down, FSL sets force the defense to make adjustments. When a formation is set to the boundary, the defense must bump its second level box players to the boundary to account for each offensive threat in that area. This creates an advantage for us because now there is more unoccupied space to the field. Running our play to the field will now give our skill players more space to operate, quickly leading to explosive plays.

If the defense fails to respect the FSL tag and does not bump its second level box players, we simply run the play to the boundary and capitalize on our numbers and leverage advantage to generate an explosive play.

## TRIPS

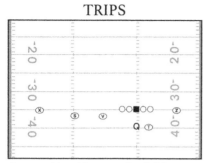

➤3-receiver side set to the field

## TRIPS FSL

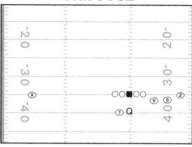

➤3-receiver side set to the boundary

*3x1 FSL Identification*

## DEUCE UP

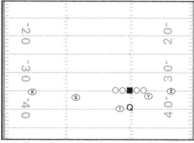

➤2 flexed vertical threats to the field; 1 to the boundary

## DEUCE UP FSL

➤2 flexed vertical threats to the boundary; 1 to the field

*2x2 FSL Identification*

## DEUCE

## DEUCE FSL

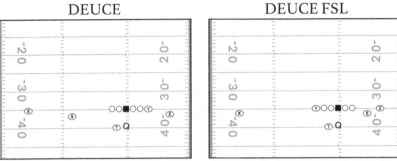

- ➢ Although the number of vertical threats to each side is equal, the number of flexed vertical threats is not
- ➢ 2 flexed vertical threats to the field; 1 to the boundary

- ➢ Although the number of vertical threats to each side is equal, the number of flexed vertical threats is not
- ➢ 2 flexed vertical threats to the boundary; 1 to the field

*2x2 FSL Identification*

## DOUBLES

## ACE

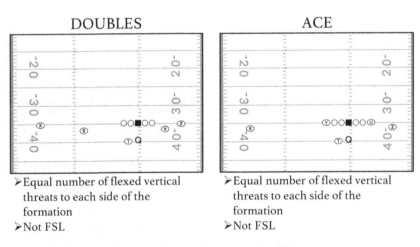

- ➢ Equal number of flexed vertical threats to each side of the formation
- ➢ Not FSL

- ➢ Equal number of flexed vertical threats to each side of the formation
- ➢ Not FSL

*2x2 FSL Identification — Not FSL*

# PRE-SNAP MOTIONS:

Pre-snap motions are an excellent way to create confusion and cause missed assignments for any defense. They force the defense to adjust on the fly which may lead to lapses in communication and critical, touchdown-conceding errors. In addition to generating defensive disorientation, we can implement pre-snap motions to limit our own mistakes on offense. By motioning before the snap, we provoke the defense into prematurely tipping its hand.

Great offensive coordinators will design pass plays that contain both a zone-beating concept and a man-beating concept. Generally, man coverage defenses require a defender to travel with the offensive player in motion, while zone defenses afford each defender the luxury of staying home. If our receiver in motion is followed by a defender, we know to throw the man-beating route concept. In contrast, if he is not followed, we hit the zone-beating concept.

This tactic converts the quarterback's and receiver's coverage read from a post-snap read to a pre-snap read. As offensive coordinators, we want to give our players as few post-snap reads as possible so that they can play fast and physical with minimal errors.

We will encounter the following pre-snap motions throughout our study of this playbook.

Across – The player in motion travels from one side of the formation to the other. Before the ball is snapped, he is allotted time to get set in his stance. These motions are generally slow in nature, and often used to change the strength of the formation in order to gain a numbers advantage over the defense.

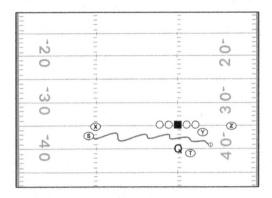

*Across Motion — Ball Is Snapped After Player Sets*

Jet – The player in motion travels full speed across the formation, but the ball is snapped while the player is still moving, either just before or just after the player crosses the face of the quarterback. The angle of this motion is generally 1 yard in front of the quarterback (or behind him if the quarterback is under center) as to either receive a jet sweep handoff or execute a fake. The purpose of this motion is to generate defensive confusion by essentially snapping the ball with an additional back in the backfield for which the defense has not had adequate time to adjust.

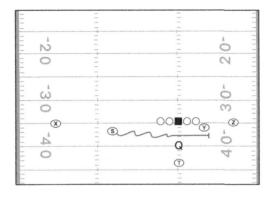

*Jet Motion — Ball Is Snapped While Player Is in Motion*

Rope – This motion only applies to players that begin their alignment in the backfield. The backfield player in motion travels at full speed out of the backfield. The ball is snapped while the back is still in motion. The word "rope" will be preceded by either a TIF (tailback into field) or TIB (tailback into boundary) acronym. These motions are designed to give us a numbers advantage on the perimeter by using the back's speed to out-leverage his man-coverage defender.

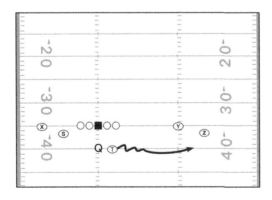

*Rope Motion — Ball Is Snapped While Player Is in Motion*

## NUMBERING THREATS:

In order to further accelerate and simplify football communication, a system was devised that identifies specific offensive threats by assigning them a numerical value. Threats are counted in ascending numerical order from outside to inside, beginning with the number 1. As we move down the line of scrimmage, the number assignations reset on the other side of the formation.

For example, Doubles has two flexed vertical threats to either side of the formation. The farthest outside threat to the strong side is #1 strong, and the next inside threat is #2 strong. To the weak side, the most outside threat is #1 weak, and the next inside threat is #2 weak.

The running back is the number 3 threat to whichever side he is aligned – strong or weak. If the running back is aligned directly behind the quarterback, he is considered the #3 receiver to both sides until he declares a side post-snap.

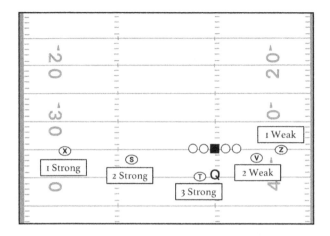

*Numbering Threats — 2x2 Formation*

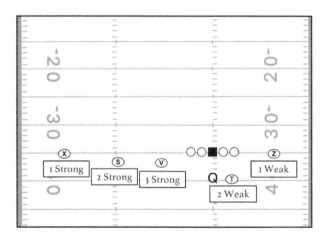

*Numbering Threats — 3x1 Formation*

# 3
# TOUCHDOWN GENIUS: RUN CONCEPTS

---

*"Throw to score; run to win."*

— COACH RON ERHARDT

---

DUE TO THE innumerable variations of defensive fronts, stunts, and blitzes, each blocking scheme must abide by certain precepts to assure success against any wrinkle the defense may throw at us. The material in this chapter will equip you and your O-line with the foundation necessary to create explosive runs through various run blocking schemes. We will analyze each run scheme featured in our 25 championship plays, divided into 2 categories: gap schemes and zone schemes.

## GAP RUN SCHEMES

Gap run schemes are designed to use an offensive lineman's leverage as his primary blocking weapon. Leverage refers to the position of the offensive lineman in correlation to the defender he will attempt to block. If the offensive tackle has a defensive end lined up on his outside shoulder, then the tackle has inside leverage on the end.

Each offensive lineman owns 2 gaps, a play side gap and a backside gap. A gap simply refers to the space between 2 blockers. To distinguish among gaps, they are assigned a letter of the alphabet. Starting at the center and moving from inside out, the gaps on either side of him are the A gaps. The next ones over are the B gaps, then the C gaps. And so it goes, down the line until we run out of blockers in the core.

A lineman's play side gap is the one on the side of the direction in which we are running the ball. His backside gap is the one on the opposite side of the direction in which we are running the ball. Therefore, if we are running the ball to the right, then the gap to the right of every offensive lineman is his play side gap, and the gap to his left is his back side gap.

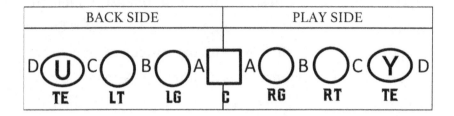

*Play Side and Back Side Gaps for a Run to the Right. Note: The gaps to the right of the back side linemen are still play side gaps as it pertains to them individually, but not as it pertains to the overall play.*

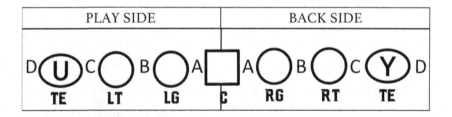

*Play Side and Back Side Gaps for a Run to the Left*

In a gap run scheme, each O-lineman will block the defender aligned in their backside gap. This is advantageous for us because we already have the correct leverage on our defenders, creating a much easier block for linemen that may struggle with the athleticism required to execute zone blocking schemes.

With the O-line all blocking down on their backside gaps, that typically leaves an unblocked defender in the farthest outside, play side gap (usually the C-gap). Depending on the defense, this unblocked C-gap defender may or may not be a defensive lineman. He may be a linebacker or even a safety. Either way, we must scheme up a way to block him or else he will make plays in the backfield all game long. To account for this, many gap schemes include one or more blockers pulling across the formation to kick out the unblocked C-gap defender. The most common pull-tactic runs are power, counter, dart, and pin & pull. The one featured in this playbook is counter.

## COUNTER:

Counter involves 2 blockers pulling across the formation. The first blocker kicks out the unblocked edge defender, and the second blocker will either wrap or insert based on the fit of the play side linebacker. If the play side backer scrapes over the top to fill the play side D-gap (outside of the kick-out block), then the second puller will wrap outside the kick-out to block him. But, if the play side backer fits in the play side C-gap (inside the kick-out block), then the second puller will insert in that gap to block him.

The non-pulling O-linemen block base gap scheme rules – blocking down on their back side gap. Even if a down-blocking O-lineman does not have a pre-snap defender aligned in his back side gap, he will still squeeze back side in case a defensive stunt or blitz brings a defender into the gap for which he is responsible. If no defenders come to rush that gap, then the O-lineman will climb to the second level and seal the back side linebacker.

To allow both pullers time to get across the formation and execute their blocks, the running back will typically take a counter step. A counter step is simply a step in the opposite direction of the play side. In addition to affording the pullers time, the counter step creates misdirection for the defense. If the linebackers react to the O-line blocking back side and the running back's first step being back side, they may overflow in that direction and be out of position when the run comes back to the play side.

The following illustrations are of a base counter scheme run to the right and run to the left, versus the same 4-2 even front. We will use this front to demonstrate the execution of each blocking scheme in this chapter and the next chapter.

*Note: In these examples, the 4-2 even front creates a 6-5 numbers advantage for the defense. This numbers disadvantage is done on purpose to allow for consistent demonstration of the maximum amount of play side blocks. Some back side defenders may be left unblocked where we would normally align a TE or FB in a real-game situation to account for the extra defender.*

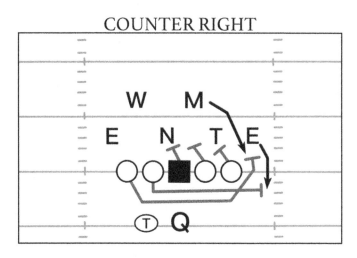

*Counter Right vs. 4-2 Even Front*

The above illustration is an example of G/T counter, a counter scheme that utilizes the back side guard and tackle as the 2 pullers.

The center and right tackle both have back side gap defenders, so they block down as indicated by our base gap scheme rules. The right guard does not have a back side gap defender, but he still steps down into that back side gap to check for a stunt or blitz.

The pulling left guard kicks out the unblocked defensive end in the play side C-gap. Now that we have an extra blocker to that side, an extra gap is created post-snap, the play side D-gap. To the play side, the C-gap is now between the right tackle and the pulling left guard, and the D-gap is to the outside of the left guard.

Having been kicked out of his original C-gap, the play side defensive end is forced to play the newly formed D-gap. The Mike linebacker – or play side backer – must fit in the play side C-gap. This causes our second puller, the left tackle, to insert instead of wrap. Had the defensive end played the C-gap, the Mike would have had to scrape over the top to fit into the D-gap, and the tackle would wrap. The second puller's ability to correctly read the fit of the play side backer, and then execute the correct blocking technique is what transforms this run scheme from a decent 1st down gain to an explosive touchdown run.

## COUNTER LEFT

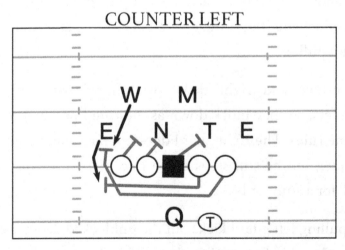

*Counter Left vs. 4-2 Even Front*

In this counter left depiction, the blocking assignments for our 2 pulling O-linemen remain the same; notice that the Will linebacker is now the play side backer.

The only O-lineman with a true back side gap defender is the left guard; he executes the gap scheme accordingly. The left tackle steps into his back side gap awaiting a stunt or blitz. The center does the same, but his rules are slightly different. With the right guard pulling, the back side A-gap is no longer between the center and right guard, it is between the center and right tackle (until he also pulls). This means that the defensive tackle aligned in right guard's back side gap pre-snap, becomes the center's closest back side gap defender post-snap. Therefore, the center must block him. This differs from the counter right scheme, in which the pulling guard and tackle does not change the fact that the nose guard is the center's closest back side gap defender.

## ZONE RUN SCHEMES

The base blocking rules of zone run schemes are the opposite of gap run schemes. Instead of blocking our back side gap defender, we will block our play side gap defender. This block is slightly more difficult to execute since we do not have the luxury of correct pre-snap leverage. However, zone schemes are extremely beneficial because they allow for double teams at the line of scrimmage, boosting the back's ability to get to the second level.

Linemen who do not have a play side gap defender will have varying responsibilities depending on which zone scheme we are running. We will discuss those details in the individual break downs that follow.

Since we are blocking play side, our back has the flexibility to read the blocks and hit whichever gap opens up. This differs from gap schemes because those runs are designed to hit between the most outside down block and the kick-out block, with the back following the wrap/insert block through the hole. In zone schemes, our backs advance through a read progression to determine which hole they will hit.

The explosive zone run schemes that we will study in this playbook are inside zone, outside zone, split zone, and zone read.

INSIDE ZONE:

Inside zone, an offensive staple across all levels of football, is designed to hit between the tackles. Standard zone blocking rules apply; the play side gaps are the priority. What makes inside zone unique is its ability to generate double teams with back side blocks. If an O-lineman does not have a play side gap defender, then he will engage in a double team by blocking down in his back side gap. Both linemen involved in the double team will then shift their eyes to the second level defenders. The lineman to whichever side the linebacker fills will abandon the double team and block the linebacker. If the defense blitzes, all double team rules are off and everyone must hold their play side gap.

There are a couple different read progressions we can use to teach the path of the running back on inside zone runs – both are effective and will depend on your back's capabilities. The first one is to read play side A-gap to backside B-gap. The perfect inside zone run will hit in the play side A-gap, but a stunting D-line may thwart our plan. If the play side A-gap is obstructed, then the back looks to wind back into the backside A-gap. If that gap is also plugged, the next read is backside B-gap. If there is still no hole, then we just get as vertical as we can and line back up for the next play.

The other read progression teaching method is to read dive to cutback to bounce. This is essentially the same as the previous method until we get to the last read. "Dive" refers to the play side A-gap. "Cutback" refers to the backside A and B gaps. And "bounce" refers to the backside C-gap, hitting the run outside of the tackles.

The first progression procedure is more effective with powerful, bruiser-style backs, while the second approach is better for speed backs. No matter which progression is taught, there is one essential rule that cannot be broken: no more than one cut behind the line of scrimmage for the running back! Inside zone is a downhill run designed to get vertical now and crease the defense – no time to waste dancing around in the backfield.

## INSIDE ZONE RIGHT

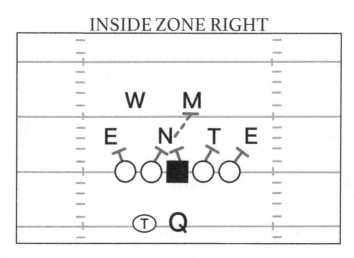

*Inside Zone Right vs. 4-2 Even Front*

Against this front, the right guard, right tackle, and left guard all have play side gap defenders. The center and left tackle do not. The center engages in a double team on the nose with the left guard. While double teaming, both o-lineman have their eyes on the play side linebacker, the Mike. If the Mike attempts to fill the play side A-gap, then the center will ditch the double team and block the Mike. If the Mike fits into the back side B-gap, then the left guard will come off the double team.

Since the back side tackle does not have a play side gap defender, nor does he have another blocker with whom to double team, he will utilize a gap hinge technique to block the back side defensive end. Gap hinge means that the O-lineman steps into his play side gap, but blocks his back side gap defender. This allows him to both protect his play side gap, and seal off the defender from chasing the play down from the back side.

The manner in which the inside zone rules block this front will provide the back with a solid play side A-gap to run through, as intended.

## INSIDE ZONE LEFT

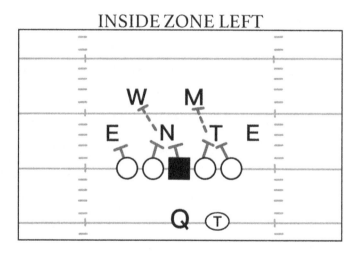

*Inside Zone Left vs. 4-2 Even Front*

As we shift the play side to the left, notice that the nature of this front allows us to generate 2 double teams. The center and both tackles have play side gap defenders. The two guards do not, so they both double team back side and look for the possibility of climbing to the play side linebacker.

The back side tackle does not gap hinge in this scenario because he has a play side gap defender.

Since the nose is being double teamed in the play side A-gap, it is likely that the back's first read will not be open. With the way our blocking rules end up playing out, this run should hit in the cutback lane, or back side A-gap.

## OUTSIDE ZONE:

Outside zone aims to attack the edge of the defense. Base zone blocking rules remain in place; we are blocking our play side gap defenders. The difference between this scheme and inside zone is the style of block utilized. On an inside zone run, O-linemen are blocking their play side gap defenders with the intention of sealing them from the inside. On an outside zone run, the O-linemen must block their play side gap defender using a reach block technique. A reach block is one in which the blocker reaches the defender's play side shoulder and seals him inside. From a viewer's perspective, it appears that all five O-linemen are running to the sideline as they attempt to gain the proper leverage to seal their defenders inside.

It is the play side tackle's job to seal the defensive end man on the line of scrimmage. If the tackle cannot seal him, then he must at least kick him out to the sideline, providing a cutback lane for the back. If an O-lineman does not have a play side gap defender, he will not double team backside like he does in inside zone. Rather, he will take 3 steps in the direction that he would have if he did have a play side gap defender. Blitzes and stunts may cause a defender to appear in this O-lineman's play side gap post-snap. If a defender does appear within those first 3 steps, then the O-lineman will take him. If not, he works to the second level and reaches the nearest play side linebacker.

The path of the running back in outside zone is the outside leg of a ghost tight end. Whoever the offensive end man on the line of scrimmage is (usually an offensive tackle), picture a tight end lined up just outside of him and aim for where that imaginary tight end's outside leg would be. This will afford the tackle enough time and space to either reach the defensive EMLOS or kick him out.

The read progression for the back is not as gap-oriented as it is in inside zone. Instead, it is block-oriented. Rather than teach the back to read play side D-gap to backside A-gap, for example. We teach him to read outside the defensive EMLOS to the back side defensive tackle. This is because the flowing nature of outside zone may appear that a gap has opened up when in reality there is a D-lineman flowing right into that "open" gap. Instead, we want to read which defenders have been successfully reached by our O-line. If the EMLOS gets reached, then we hit the outside immediately. If not, we read the next block, and so on and so forth until we find a reached defender.

## OUTSIDE ZONE RIGHT

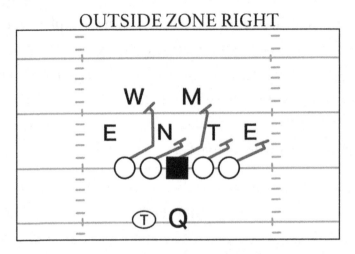

*Outside Zone Right vs. 4-2 Even Front*

The defensive EMLOS is the play side defensive end, so that is who the right tackle needs to reach. Both of the guards are responsible for reaching their play side gap defenders. The center and left tackle both take 3 steps play side at the snap of the ball, no defenders enter their play side gaps so they each climb to the nearest play side backer. The unblocked back side defensive end should not be able to chase this play down from the back side. But if he can, we can adjust the back side tackle's block to a gap hinge as long as he does not have a play side gap defender.

Since the right tackle is the offensive EMLOS (excluding flexed receivers), the back's path is the outside leg of the ghost tight end, or in other words, the imaginary play side D-gap.

## OUTSIDE ZONE LEFT

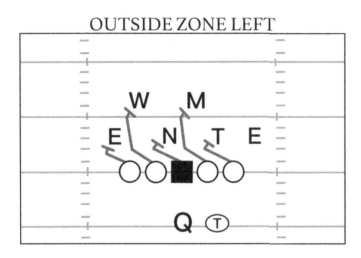

*Outside Zone Left vs. 4-2 Even Front*

As we run this play to the left side, the defensive EMLOS remains the play side defensive end; it is now the left tackle's responsibility to reach him. Our other two O-linemen with play side gap defenders are the center and right tackle. Both guards will take their 3 play side steps looking for work. If work does not come to them naturally, then they will find it by climbing to the nearest play side linebacker.

The back's path remains the imaginary play side D-gap.

## SPLIT ZONE:

The remaining zone schemes are all appendages to either inside zone or outside zone. Split zone most commonly features an inside zone blocking scheme, although it may also be paired with outside zone. The defining characteristic of split zone is the usage of an additional blocker, aligned in the backfield, who comes from the play side to perform a bang block on the back side EMLOS. This extra backfield blocker is referred to as a splitter.

Since the splitter's responsibility is the back side EMLOS, the back side tackle does not need to gap hinge if he does not have a play side gap defender. Instead, he can immediately climb to the second level and cut off the nearest play side linebacker.

Depending on the front, split zone allows us to either gain an extra double team or climb to the second level more quickly while still blocking the back side EMLOS. The split zone read progression for the running back is the same as it is for the base zone scheme that we are running, either inside zone or outside zone.

## SPLIT ZONE RIGHT

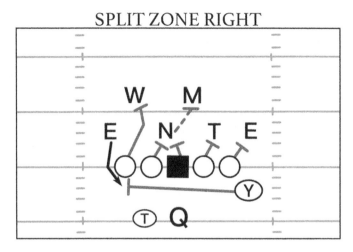

*Split Zone Right vs. 4-2 Even Front*

The blocking scheme is the same as inside zone right, with the exception of the left tackle. Instead of performing a gap hinge, he immediately climbs to seal the Will, his nearest play side backer.

The splitter, in this case, is a tight end. He is positioned in a two-point stance, about 1 yard behind the right tackle, aligning his inside foot with the tackle's outside foot. At the snap of the ball, he shoots across the formation, staying tight to the line of scrimmage, and kicks out the crashing defensive end.

## SPLIT ZONE LEFT

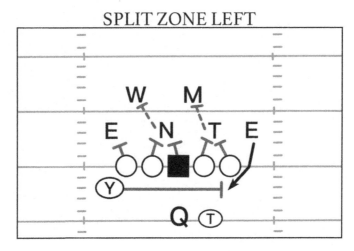

*Split Zone Left vs. 4-2 Even Front*

Now that we are running to the left, the right tackle has a play side gap defender. Therefore, the back side defensive end will be unblocked regardless of which zone scheme we are running. This is why split zone is so effective; we are able to block the back side defensive end and still have two double teams at the line of scrimmage.

ZONE READ:

Zone read schemes offer the same benefits as split zone without the need for an additional blocker. Instead of blocking the back side EMLOS with a splitter, zone read schemes require us to read that defender. This means that what we do on a zone read scheme will be dictated by the post-snap decision of the read defender.

As the quarterback and running back enter the handoff mesh point – the time during a handoff in which both the running back and the quarterback have hands on the football – the quarterback has his eyes on the read defender. If the read defender crashes to tackle the running back, then the quarterback pulls the ball from the mesh point and hits the backside C-gap. If the read defender stays home, waiting for the quarterback pull, then we give the ball to the running back and execute the base zone scheme that was called.

Since we can convert any zone scheme into a zone read, we need to tag the read option to a base zone blocking scheme such as inside zone or outside zone. The only thing that changes for the O-line is that the back side tackle will not gap hinge the back side EMLOS, since that will be our read defender. The rest of the O-line executes the base rules of the called zone scheme.

Read plays are an excellent way to gain a numbers advantage in the run game since they force the defense to commit a defender to playing the quarterback. They also allow us to run the ball effectively even if we are at a numbers disadvantage because we do not have to spare a blocker on the read defender.

## INSIDE ZONE READ RIGHT

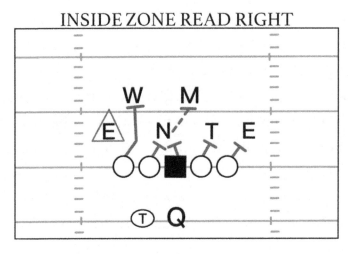

*Inside Zone Read Right vs. 4-2 Even Front*

## INSIDE ZONE READ LEFT

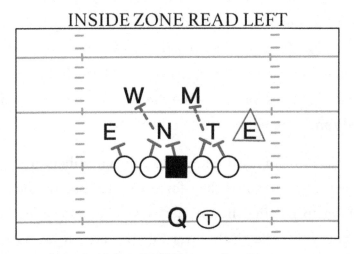

*Inside Zone Read Left vs. 4-2 Even Front*

In both of these examples, the read defender is the back side defensive end. By reading this defender, we are able to account for every box defender, even though we have 1 less blocker. These schemes are excellent ways to put defenders in conflict and accentuate the athleticism and talents of a dual-threat quarterback.

———

Both gap schemes and zone schemes provide us with unique advantages that will produce a relentless ground attack. The challenge is learning to use these schemes most effectively. As we progress into this playbook, we will examine *when*, *how*, and *why* the college football geniuses utilize these same concepts to win championships at the highest levels.

# 4

# TOUCHDOWN GENIUS: PASS PROTECTIONS

---

*"Football is not a contact sport; it is a collision sport."*

— COACH DUFFY DAUGHERTY

---

OUR ABILITY TO protect in the passing game is equally vital to our championship potential as our dominance in the run game. Throughout this playbook, we will study 2 main protection schemes: half slide and full slide. Each of these slide protections will differ slightly depending on the number of blockers we include in the protection; this playbook showcases 5-man, 6-man, and 7-man protections.

## HALF SLIDE:

Half slide protection indicates that some of the offensive linemen will slide to the back side and execute a zone protection scheme, while the remaining O-linemen block their defenders man-to-man. Those who are included in the slide, are responsible for blocking their gap in the direction of which they are sliding, or in other words, their back side gap. Which offensive linemen slide and which ones block man-to-man will be determined by both the offensive play call and the defensive front.

Protection schemes are often manifest as 2-digit numbers. The first number reveals the number of blockers in the protection, and the second number denotes the play side and protection type; even numbers indicate plays to the right and odd numbers to the left. Contrary to run schemes, a pass play called to the right will not always go to the right. There are many other pre- and post-snap variables that will determine where the ball actually goes. Nonetheless, assigning a play side and back side to a pass play allows everybody involved in the protection (quarterback included) to be on the same page. The man side will always be called to the play side, and the half slide will always be assigned to the back side.

Consider the following half slide protection examples.

50 – 5-man protection; man to the right, half slide to the left

51 – 5-man protection; man to the left, half slide to the right

60 – 6-man protection; man to the right, half slide to the left

61 – 6-man protection; man to the left, half slide to the right

Now that we've clarified each side's responsibility in a half slide scheme, let's discuss how we determine exactly how many linemen will participate in the slide. To do this, we must first understand how to use defensive line techniques to recognize the difference between covered and uncovered linemen.

A D-lineman's technique refers to his pre-snap alignment. The following diagram depicts all of the possible D-line techniques.

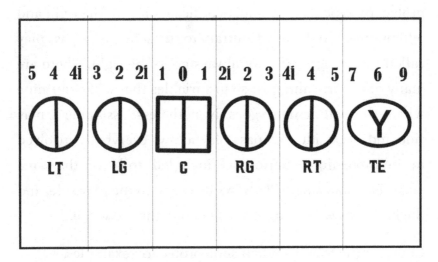

*D-Line Techniques*

Each number represents a potential defensive lineman if he were aligned where the number is positioned. 0, 2, 4, and 6 techniques are D-linemen aligned head up on their respective O-linemen. 2i, 4i, and 7 techniques depict inside shades. 1, 3, 5, and 9 techniques reveal outside shades.

An offensive lineman is uncovered if he does not have a defensive lineman aligned in any of the three techniques within the framework of his body. For example, if the closest D-linemen to the right guard are aligned in a 1 technique (also referred to as a shade) and a 4i technique, then he is uncovered. But say the 4i technique shifts to a 3 technique; now the right guard is covered to the outside.

This knowledge is essential to performing half slide protection. Versus a 3-down defensive front, the first uncovered offensive lineman will initiate the slide. Against a 4-down front, the slide is initiated by the first open play side gap (counting from the outside in). So, if the play side A gap is the first open gap, then the center will initiate the slide. Everyone to the back side of the slide-initiating lineman will slide, and everybody to the play slide of the slide-initiator will block man-to-man. This will generally result in either a 3-man slide initiated by the center, or a 4-man slide initiated by the play side guard, but it is possible to have a 5-man slide once we get into 7-man protections. If the back is included in the protection, then he will provide help and/or blitz pick-up to the man side.

## 50 vs. 4-DOWN

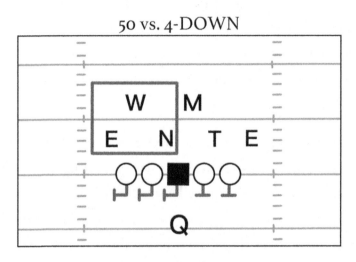

*50 Pass Protection vs. 4-Down Even Front*

The even number play call designates the right side as the play side. Since we are facing a 4-down front, we will use open play side gaps as the slide initiator. The play side C-gap is covered by the 5 technique, and the play side B-gap by the 3 technique. The right tackle and right guard both have man-to-man responsibility. Our first uncovered play side gap is the A-gap, so every offensive lineman to the back side of that A-gap is going to slide back side, which, in this case, is to the left.

The grey box enclosing the nose guard, back side defensive end, and Will linebacker indicates the three defenders that our 3-man slide is responsible for blocking. They are each responsible for their back side gap, regardless of which of those three defenders attempts to penetrate it.

Seeing that we have a 5-man protection called versus a 6-man box, the defense is able to blitz one more defender than we are able to block. That extra defender is who the quarterback is going to read. In this case, it's the Mike linebacker. If the Mike linebacker blitzes, then the quarterback knows that he needs to throw his hot route to avoid taking a sack. If the Mike drops into coverage, then we can execute the drop back pass concept as called because we know that we at least have 5-on-5.

## 50 vs. 3-DOWN

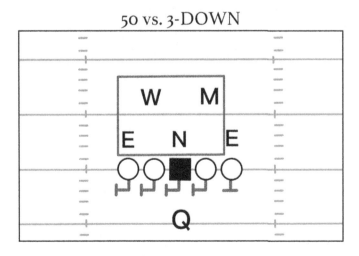

*50 Pass Protection vs. 3-Down Odd Front*

Notice how the same protection call changes versus a 3-down front. Our 3-down front rules state that the first uncovered offensive lineman initiates the slide. This results in a 4-man slide instead of a 3-man. The play side tackle remains covered as he now faces a 4 technique. But the play side guard does not have any body directly over him or shaded to either side; he is uncovered. So, the play side guard initiates the slide, giving us four zone defenders on the defenses four potential pass rushers enclosed in the grey box.

## 51 vs. 4-DOWN

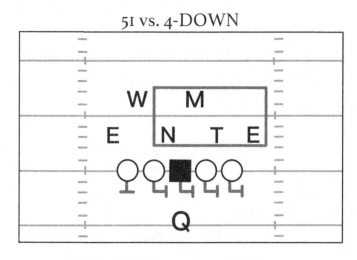

*51 Pass Protection vs. 4-Down Even Front*

Returning to our 5-man protection versus an even front, see how the protection changes by shifting the play side from the right to the left, running 51 instead of 50.

Notice how we still end up with a 4-man slide, even though the defense is in a 4-down front. The play side C-gap is covered, but the B-gap is not. Therefore, our slide starts with the left guard, providing a 4-on-4 zone match up to the slide side. The Will is now the quarterback's hot read since he is the extra defender for which our 5-man protection cannot account.

Evidently, 5-man half slide protection is not ideal against a 6-man front. That is why they are best suited for quick game – 1-step drop throws intended to get the ball out of the quarterback's hands quickly and efficiently. But let's take a look at how we can improve our half slide scheme by introducing a sixth protector into the mix. This tactic is much more effective to protect our quarterback long enough to connect on a deep shot down the field.

## 60 vs. 4-DOWN

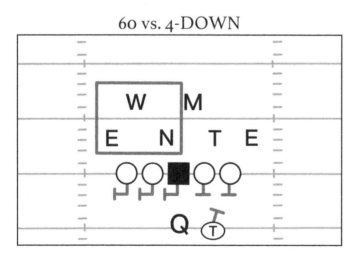

*60 Pass Protection vs. 4-Down Even Front*

Our sixth protector in this scenario is the running back. As previously stated, the back's responsibility in half slide protection is to help the man side and pick up any blitzing defenders that may slip through. Even if the back is aligned to the back side, he will cross the quarterback's face post-snap to help with the man concept on the play side.

In 50 protection, the quarterback must read the Mike linebacker to decide whether or not he needs to throw hot. Now that our back has blitz pick-up responsibility, the quarterback does not need to make a hot read versus a 6-man box; he can execute the pass concept as designed. If the defense brings a Sam linebacker into the box as a seventh defender, then the quarterback's hot read is back on. The back and the quarterback will read both the Mike and Sam linebackers. If just one of them blitzes, we are fine because we still have 6-on-6. If they both blitz, then the back will pick up the inside blitzer – who is the most dangerous – and the quarterback will throw hot.

The following illustrations depict the protection schemes 61, 70, and 71, all versus a 4-down front. Notice how the core O-line assignments do not change as we add blockers in the protection. 50, 60, and 70 are all blocked the same by our five offensive linemen.

## 61 vs. 4-Down

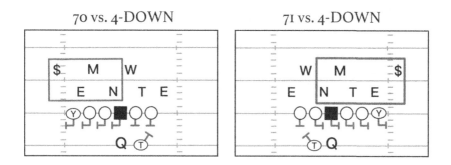

*61 Pass Protection vs. 4-Down Even Front*

### 70 vs. 4-DOWN

### 71 vs. 4-DOWN

*70 & 71 Pass Protections vs. 4-Down Even Front*

FULL SLIDE:

In a full slide protection scheme, every offensive lineman will slide to the back side. Doing so will leave the play side C-gap exposed to any type of edge rush. To protect against this, we use tight ends and backs to replace the back side tackle and hold that C-gap. For this reason, full slide protection is most commonly utilized as a 6- or 7-man scheme. In full slide protection, we do not need to worry about whether an O-lineman is covered or uncovered since everybody will be sliding back side regardless.

## 68 vs. 4-DOWN

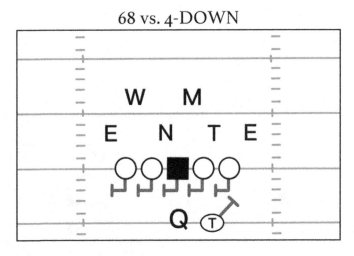

*68 Pass Protection vs. 4-Down Even Front*

Consider this 6-man full slide protection, which we will call 68.

The number 6 indicates a 6-man protection, and the even number, 8, declares the play side to the right while indicating full slide protection (8 and 9 are personal preference numbers to dictate full slide, while 0 and 1 are personal preference to dictate half slide; you should use whichever identification works the best for your team). Since the play side is to the right, and the O-line's responsibility is to slide back side, everyone will slide to their left. With the right tackle being the offensive EMLOS, the play side C-gap is vacated. The back inserts himself right off the outside hip of the right tackle to take that gap.

## 78 vs. 4-DOWN

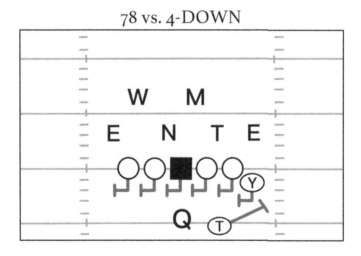

*78 Pass Protection vs. 4-Down Even Front*

Now that we have a tight end in the above protection, it becomes a 7-man scheme. The tight end will slide into the play side C-gap. The vacated edge gap is now the play side D-gap, which is where the back will insert and pick up any edge pressure.

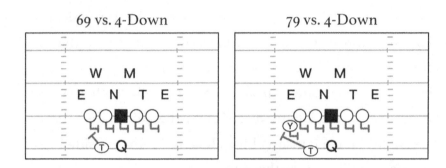

*69 & 79 Pass Protections vs. 4-Down Even Front*

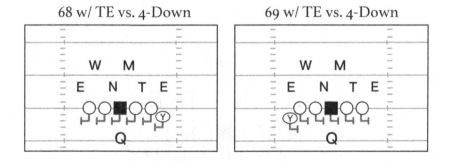

*68 & 69 Pass Protections vs. 4-Down Even Front — Full Slide Protections with No Running Back Involved*

Now that we have established the terminology, base run concepts, and base pass protections that will be the foundation for this winning playbook, we are ready to see them in actions as we dive deep into the analysis of our 25 championship scoring plays.

# +35 YARD SCORING RUNS

# 1

## INSIDE ZONE
### 2017 SEC CHAMPIONSHIP
### GEORGIA BULLDOGS VS. AUBURN TIGERS

**— CHAMPION —**
**GEORGIA BULLDOGS**

# INSIDE ZONE

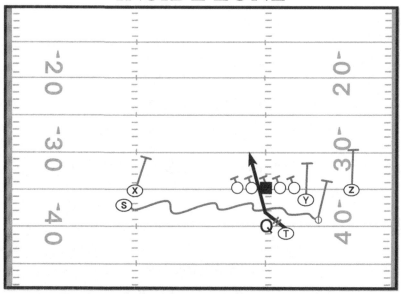

| POSITION | ALIGNMENT | ASSIGNMENT | COACHING NOTE |
|---|---|---|---|
| Q | GUN | HANDOFF TO T | WAIT FOR S TO SET BEFORE SNAP; CARRYOUT IZ READ FAKE AFTER HANDOFF |
| T | BEHIND OG; TOES TO HEELS | READ: PS-A, BS-A, BS-C | NO MORE THAN 1 CUT BEHIND LOS |
| X | FIELD HASH | BLOCK HEAD UP DB | RUN DB OFF IF PRESSED |
| Z | BOUND. BOT. #s | BLOCK BC | RUN DB OFF IF PRESSED |
| S | HASH +1 | SAC MOTION; BLOCK FS | SET AFTER MOTION IN WR STANCE; 1 YD O.S. Y, 1 YD BEHIND LOS |
| Y | I.S./O.S.; TOES TO HEELS | INSIDE ZONE LT | WING STANCE/2 PT. STANCE - FEET SQUARE TO LOS, NO HAND ON THE GROUND |
| OL | BASE | INSIDE ZONE LT | PS GAP 1ST RESPONSIBILITY; NO DBL TEAM VS. BLITZ |

## FORMATION: GS TREY UP FSL
## PERSONNEL: 11
## MOTION: S-ACROSS

### SCHEME:

Inside zone is a great base down (1st and 2nd down) call. It is typical of defensive coordinators to play base defense on base downs and then showcase their blitz packages on 3rd down. Since inside zone permits us to double team one or more defensive linemen, we should be able to consistently gain positive yards against any base defense on this play, allowing us to expand our playbook on subsequent downs.

The Georgia Bulldogs provide us with an excellent example of maximizing the potential of even the simplest run scheme. When designing run plays, our job is to draw up a scheme that puts the running back in a 1-on-1 situation with the safety, affording him the best opportunity to create an explosive play. Georgia's offense does exactly that on this inside zone run.

### PRE-SNAP:

While it may seem counterproductive to run away from the strength of the formation, there is great value in using space to our advantage. Georgia utilizes two pre-snap tactics to force defenders into the boundary and create wide open space to the field. These tactics are FSL and pre-snap motion.

As discussed in chapter 2, FSL formations force the defense to adjust and match personnel to the boundary, leaving the offense plenty of space to work with to the field. Georgia's formation does not actually become FSL until after the SAC motion occurs. This formational shift applies pressure on the defense to adjust to the FSL set quicker than they are comfortable with, providing us the mismatches that we are seeking.

Auburn's defense is playing Cover 1 Hole, a man coverage scheme including zone help from a deep post player and a shallow hole player.

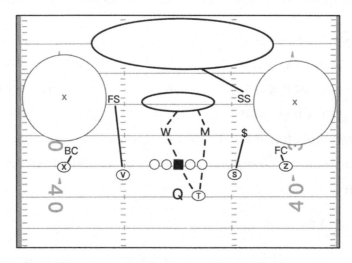

*Cover 1 Hole vs. Doubles. Note: All coverage images will feature Doubles to best illustrate base coverage rules. Circles with an "x" at the center indicate coverage weakness zone*

The Tigers run this out of a 4-2-5 package – 4 defensive linemen, 2 linebackers, and 5 defensive backs. The 2 zone players in this defense are determined by the formation of the offense. Remember, up tight ends are non-vertical threats regarded by defenses as an extra back in the backfield. By placing the up tight end into the boundary, Georgia causes Auburn to bring their free safety down into the box at linebacker depth to respect the run threat that the tight end poses. This weak-side rotation places the strong safety in the post, thus withdrawing a defender from the wide side of the field.

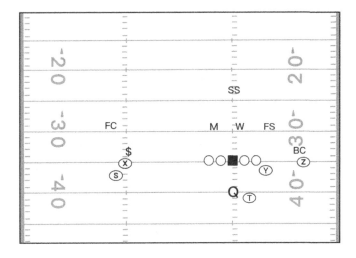

*Cover 1 Weak Side Safety Rotation vs. GS Trey Up FSL (pre-SAC motion)*

As Georgia's slot receiver motions into the boundary, he converts the formation to FSL, while also changing the strength of the formation. This causes the linebackers to shift slightly further into the boundary, while also bringing over another man-coverage defender.

When defenses play single high safety, man-to-man defense, many of them will respond to formation-crossing motions by jumping them. This means that when the offensive player in motion crosses the quarterback's face, the post player jumps down to play him man-to-man, and the previous man defender jumps back, becoming the post player.

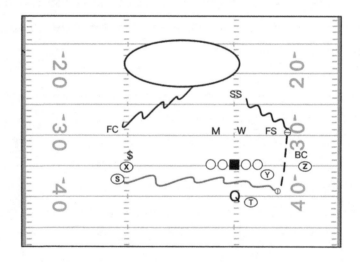

*Man-to-Man Coverage Jump Technique*

By utilizing the SAC motion, the field corner and strong safety jump the motion, placing the safety in the boundary and the corner in the post, subtracting yet another Auburn defender from the field. Georgia has now taken Auburn's better run support player out of the post and replaced him with a lesser-tackling corner.

## POST-SNAP:

The Tiger's defensive line is set in an under front, consisting of the following D-line techniques: field 5, 3, 1 (shade), and boundary 5. In an under front, the 3 technique is set to the opposite side of the tight end, and the shade is to tight end's side. With Georgia aligning their tight end in the boundary, Auburn's under front sets the 3 technique to the field.

Against this front, Georgia's left guard and left tackle both have defenders in their play side gaps, so they block them 1-on-1. The center does not have a play side gap defender since the nose is shaded to the boundary. This allows him to double team the nose with the right guard, creating a wide-open, play side A-gap for Georgia's back to run through.

Under and over fronts (over being the opposite of under – 3 technique set to the same side as the tight end), are primarily 11 and 12 personnel calls for the defense. Although Georgia runs away from the tight end on this play, his mere presence is enough to manipulate the defense for a 64-yard touchdown. Everything that we do must serve a purpose, even the most mundane matters such as personnel placement can be the difference between winning and losing.

ADJUSTMENTS:

One of the more difficult tasks across all levels of football is downfield blocking. As a large portion of this play's explosiveness relies on a solid downfield block by the X receiver, we can make adjustments as needed. Georgia aligns their X on the field hash; but since the purpose of this play is to create space to the field, we may widen our X all the way out to the field numbers. This will create an almost insurmountable distance for the field corner to travel to make the tackle should the X fail to block him.

Another adjustment we can make if our receivers struggle to block on the perimeter is to run off the DBs rather than block them. This alteration applies to man coverage only. Man coverage results in the defenders playing with their eyes glued to their threat. By running off our man-coverage defenders, we take them out of the run fit without needing to block them.

# 2

## OUTSIDE ZONE READ

### 2018 ACC CHAMPIONSHIP

### CLEMSON TIGERS VS. PITTSBURGH PANTHERS

**— CHAMPION —**

**CLEMSON TIGERS**

# OUTSIDE ZONE READ

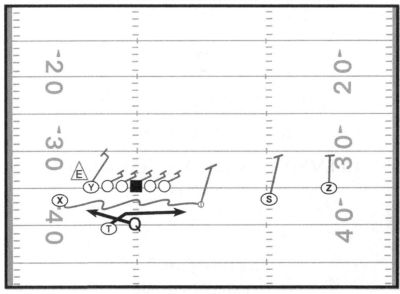

| POSITION | ALIGNMENT | ASSIGNMENT | COACHING NOTE |
|---|---|---|---|
| Q | GUN | READ: EMLOS | CRASH = PULL, STAY = HANDOFF; CARRYOUT OZ READ FAKE IF GIVE |
| T | SPLIT OG/OT; 1 YD BEHIND QB | READ: PS-D TO I.S. BLOCKS | READ BLOCKS, NOT GAPS; HIT OFF THE PS SHOULDER PAD OF 1ST OL TO REACH DL |
| X | BOUND. TOP #s | XAC MOTION; BLOCK NICKEL | SET AFTER MOTION, DIVIDE HASH & OT; BLOCK O.S. SHOULDER OF NICKEL |
| Z | FIELD TOP #s | BLOCK FC | RUN DB OFF IF PRESSED |
| S | FIELD HASH | BLOCK SS | BLOCK O.S. SHOULDER OF SS |
| Y | EOL | LEAVE EMLOS; BLOCK 2ND LEVEL | 3 PT. STANCE; SEAL OFF BACKSIDE FLOW, MAKE DEFENDER GO UNDERNEATH BLOCK |
| OL | BASE | OUTSIDE ZONE RT | REACH PS DEFENDER; WORK TO 2ND LEVEL IF FREE; HEAD UP DEFENDER = PS DEFENDER |

**FORMATION: GS TRIPS CLOSED**
**PERSONNEL: 11**
**MOTION: X-ACROSS**

## SCHEME:

Zone read schemes are also solid base down calls due to their effectiveness against base defenses. On $1^{st}$ and $2^{nd}$ down, defensive coordinators are primarily concerned with stopping the run, hoping to force the offense into a must-throw $3^{rd}$ & long situation. When the defense blitzes, they sacrifice their ability to play on different levels. Just one missed assignment or missed tackle, and the running back could get to the secondary untouched for an explosive run.

While blitzing does expose the defense to the possibility of being gashed, it would not bode well for us on this particular play. Blitz schemes feature a running back blitzer and a quarterback blitzer. Since the quarterback can only read what is transpiring on the back side, we are susceptible to any play side pressure that may be coming.

While we must be careful to avoid this call on our opponents' blitz-happy down & distance, Clemson demonstrates exactly how lethal it can be against a base defense.

## PRE-SNAP:

The XAC motion on this play performs multiple functions. Since this is a zone read, the motion needs to serve both of the quarterback's options in the read. The Panthers are in zone coverage, so nobody follows the motion to the other side of the formation. By motioning the X to the field, Clemson provides an extra perimeter blocker should the quarterback's read dictate an outside zone handoff. The X's departure also serves to create space in the boundary for the potential quarterback keep.

The pre-snap read for the quarterback is the boundary EMLOS. In this case, the defensive end aligned outside the Y in a 9 technique. If the DE crashes, the quarterback will keep it. And if he stays home, the quarterback will execute the handoff to the running back.

POST-SNAP:

Clemson's O-line and running back provide a textbook example of outside zone as the read defender plays the quarterback and forces the handoff. Pitt's D-line plays an over front, so the 3 technique is set to the tight end on the back side. This gives the right tackle a field 5 technique lined up in his play side gap. He fails to reach block him, but he is able to successfully kick him out and provide the back with a cutback lane.

The right guard has no play side gap defender, so he takes his 3 lateral steps and then works up to the second level to seal the Mike linebacker. The center, who does have a shade defender aligned in his play side gap, fails to reach the slanting nose guard, so he kicks out as well. The left guard has no play side gap responsibility; he works to the second level and seals the Will linebacker after his 3 lateral steps.

Finally, we get a successful reach block with the left tackle on the boundary 3 technique. The back gets vertical off the left tackle's right shoulder pad and is able to immediately bounce back outside thanks to the 2 guards sealing second level defenders. A couple of perimeter blocks later by the 2 slot receivers and Clemson has themselves a 75-yard touchdown run.

Had Clemson elected to forgo the XAC motion to the field, the S would have had to choose between blocking Pitt's nickel and safety. This would have given Pitt a free defender to come down and make the tackle. But, since the X motioned to #3 strong, he was able to block the nickel while the S worked up to the safety. These 2 blocks ended up being the difference between 2 & 7 and a touchdown for the Tigers.

ADJUSTMENTS:

If we are participating in a level of football in which zone reads are too difficult on the quarterback, we can easily convert this play into either regular outside zone or a designed QB keep and still produce the same result. To do this, we just need to adjust the TE's responsibility in the blocking scheme.

To run regular outside zone, the TE will have the same responsibility as the rest of the OL. Against this front, he does not have a play side gap defender, so he will take his 3 lateral steps and then work to seal a second level defender. He does not need to gap hinge the defensive end, as a 9 technique should not be able to chase an automatic-give outside zone run down from the back side.

To convert this play into an automatic QB keep, the TE will block the DE. The QB will fake the outside zone handoff and hit either the boundary C- or D-gap (depending on the TE's block). This will put the quarterback 1-on-1 in space with the corner. If the D-line does not adjust their front to align outside of the TE, then the QB keep is a touchdown all day.

# 3

# SPLIT ZONE BLUFF READ

## 2021 BIG 10 CHAMPIONSHIP

## MICHIGAN WOLVERINES VS. IOWA HAWKEYES

— CHAMPION —

**MICHIGAN WOLVERINES**

# SPLIT ZONE BLUFF READ

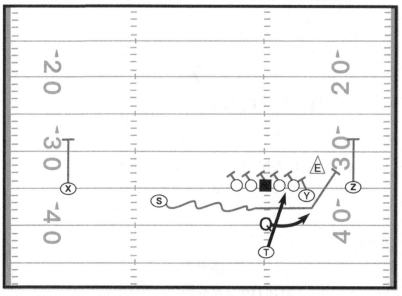

| POSITION | ALIGNMENT | ASSIGNMENT | COACHING NOTE |
|----------|-----------|------------|---------------|
| Q | GUN | READ: EMLOS | CRASH = PULL & FOLLOW S, STAY = HANDOFF; CARRYOUT FAKE IF HANDOFF; MESH POINT RT |
| T | PISTOL; 2 YDS BEHIND QB | READ: PS-A, BS-A, BS-C | PS TO THE FIELD (LT), MESH POINT TO THE RT |
| X | FIELD TOP #s | BLOCK FC | RUN DB OFF IF PRESSED |
| Z | BOUND. BOT. #s | BLOCK BC | RUN DB OFF IF PRESSED |
| S | FIELD HASH - 2 | JET MOTION; BLUFF EMLOS; LEAD FOR QB | BECOME LEAD BLOCKER AFTER BLUFF, KICK OUT O.S. MDM |
| Y | I.S./O.S.; TOES TO HEELS | SPLIT ZONE LT | IF UNCOVERED PS, NO BS GAP HINGE, LEAVE EMLOS & WORK TO 2ND LEVEL (I.S. MDM) |
| OL | BASE | SPLIT ZONE LT | BLOCK THE SAME AS IZ LT W/ NO GAP HINGE; Y RESPONSIBLE FOR LEAVING EMLOS |

**FORMATION: PISTOL DEUCE UP**
**PERSONNEL: 11**
**MOTION: S-JET**

## SCHEME:

As this play is built off of a couple different schemes, it will be most effective when it is correctly set up. The two plays that will set this play up well are jet sweep and split zone. The strategy of this play is to put the EMLOS in conflict so we can run behind a lead blocker no matter what the quarterback's read indicates.

Versus a jet sweep, defensive edge players are instructed to hit the jet and cancel out that portion of the play regardless of whether or not he is even handed the ball. Utilizing the jet player as the split zone bang blocker entices the EMLOS to come up-field, when in reality, his split zone responsibility is to spill (get underneath) the block. After running several true jet sweeps and jet motion split zone concepts, the EMLOS will be in conflict before the ball is even snapped on this split zone bluff read.

## PRE-SNAP:

The pre-snap jet motion causes Iowa's box defenders to overcommit to their outside flow, putting them outside of their designated run fits. If we have set this play up correctly, the EMLOS has a decision to make once he sees jet motion. Is he going to play the jet sweep or the split zone?

The Hawkeyes are playing Cover 3 Weak, a zone coverage scheme beginning with a 2-high safety shell but rotating to the weak side to reveal single-high Cover 3 post-snap.

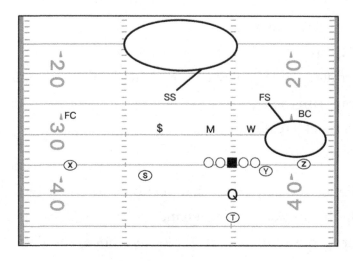

*Cover 3 Weak Safety Post-Snap Rotation*

Once the weak side safety rotates down, he becomes the force player in the run fit, responsible for forcing the ball back into the teeth of the defense. In addition to having a force player, every run fit should also have a plug player, who is responsible for playing inside out. As we will see in our post-snap analysis, Michigan's jet action on this play causes a run fit breakdown between Iowa's force and plug players.

## POST-SNAP:

At the snap of the ball, the defensive end flies up-field to play the jet, indicating an easy give read for the QB. Required to respect the possibility of jet sweep, the force player maintains hard outside leverage and does his job forcing the ball back inside. However, the defense is missing its plug player, the Mike linebacker. The Mike over-flows outside with the jet and leaves a massive gap for Michigan's back to exploit.

While the S-jet motion plays a pivotal role in setting up this explosive run, the real genius of this play lies in what the jet receiver does post-snap. Rather than bang block the EMLOS like true split zone, the S bluffs the bang block and becomes the lead blocker for the quarterback should his read prompt him to keep the ball. In this case, the QB hands it off to the back, but the lead blocker is still put to good use. The back makes one cut behind the line of scrimmage and hits the back side C-gap (back side because the OL is blocking split zone left). By the time he gets to Iowa's last line of defense, our lead-blocking slot receiver is there to make the 67-yard touchdown-sealing block.

## ADJUSTMENTS:

As with our previous zone read scheme, we can convert this play into an automatic give to take away the read aspect from the quarterback. The blocking scheme does not change, since the bluff block will be sufficient to freeze the EMLOS long enough for the back to hit the hole. If the EMLOS is not buying the bluff block, we can still be successful running true split zone out of this look and bang blocking with the S-jet receiver.

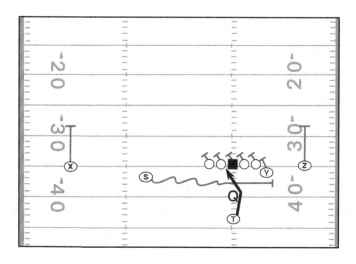

*Split Zone Bluff Read Adjustment — S-Jet Split Zone*

# 4

## FAKE TOSS QB COUNTER

### 2020 ACC CHAMPIONSHIP

### CLEMSON TIGERS VS. NOTRE DAME FIGHTING IRISH

**— CHAMPION —**
**CLEMSON TIGERS**

# FAKE TOSS QB COUNTER

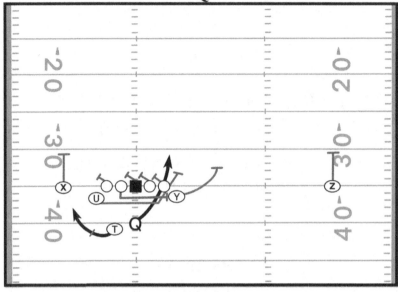

| POSITION | ALIGNMENT | ASSIGNMENT | COACHING NOTE |
|---|---|---|---|
| Q | GUN | FAKE TOSS; RUN COUNTER | BE PATIENT & ALLOW PULLERS TO GET ACROSS BEFORE RUNNING THE COUNTER |
| T | SPLIT OG/OT, 1.5 YDS BEHIND QB | FAKE TOSS | SELL FAKE, GET VERTICAL AT LEAST 5 YDS UP-FIELD |
| X | BOUND. TOP #s | BLOCK BC | RUN DB OFF IF PRESSED |
| Z | FIELD TOP #s | BLOCK FC | RUN DB OFF IF PRESSED |
| Y | I.S./O.S.; 2 YDS BEHIND OT | REACH BLOCK 2ND LEVEL DEFENDER | ARC RELEASE - LOOP O.S. ON REACH BLOCK; WIDEN RUNNING LANE FOR PULLERS AND QB |
| U | I.S./O.S.; 2 YDS BEHIND OT | PULL & WRAP/INSERT | READ MIKE LB'S FIT TO DETERMINE WRAP VS. INSERT; FILL = INSERT, SCRAPE = WRAP |
| OL | BASE | G/U COUNTER; BSG PULL & KICK | BSG KICK OUT PS EMLOS; BST GAP HINGE PS TO HELP CENTER CANCEL BSG'S VACATED GAP |

**FORMATION: ACE UP**
**PERSONNEL: 12**
**MOTION: N/A**

SCHEME:

So far, we have witnessed each of our chapter 3 zone schemes in action. Clemson's Fake Toss QB Counter displays our first championship gap run scheme. As opposed to the previous runs we have studied this chapter, this is an excellent 3$^{rd}$ down run. Gap schemes are great against the blitz because they cancel out back side gaps while bringing extra blockers to the play side. Whether the defense brings a back side or front side blitz, we have an answer.

The key to canceling back side gaps in a counter run scheme is utilizing a TE as one of the pullers. By doing so on this play, Clemson's left tackle can help the center cancel the pulling guard's vacated gap, while also maintaining his own gap integrity. The way he does this is by gap hinging into his play side gap.

PRE-SNAP:

There is nothing fancy about this pre-snap action. The Tigers find themselves in a 3$^{rd}$ & 1 situation and their answer is to line up in 12 personnel and run the ball right at the Fighting Irish.

Clemson's balanced formation provides play direction ambiguity for the defense. Defending out of a Cover 1 look, Notre Dame must bring 2 additional, second level defenders into the box – now totaling 4 – to account for the 3 players in Clemson's backfield. Without a true run strength, there is no pre-snap indication of where the ball may be heading, and the 4 second-level defenders must rely solely on post-snap reads.

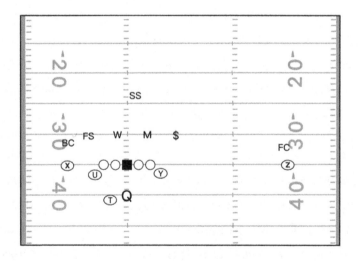

*Cover 1 Adjustment to 3 Backfield Threats*

## POST-SNAP:

The blocking scheme on this play is base counter, featuring the back side guard and tight end as the 2 pullers. The guard executes the kick-out block and the tight end handles the wrap/insert. Aligned in an over front, Notre Dame does Clemson a huge favor by slanting their D-line into the backside gaps of the O-line. As the 3 technique slants out of the right tackle's gap and into the right guard's gap, the right tackle can now work up to the second level and seal the Will linebacker (leave the Mike for the pulling TE). The stunting field 5 technique forces the Mike backer to scrape over the top and fill the play side D-gap. As his read dictates, the pulling TE wraps and does an excellent job eliminating the Mike linebacker as the run creases through the play side D-gap.

While Clemson's front seven execute this counter scheme to near perfection, it is the fake toss that elevates it from a 1st down to a 34-yard touchdown. The play fake needs to last long enough to both be convincing and allow the pullers time to get across the formation. Down 17 points in the ACC Championship game, Notre Dame's post safety was desperate to come down hill and get the ball back to his offense. However, his overzealousness to make a play misled him into biting hard on the fake toss and he was out of his designated last-line-of-defense safety position. Once the pullers fulfilled their responsibilities, the defense had no chance at catching the quarterback.

## ADJUSTMENTS:

Not every team has the luxury of operating comfortably out of 12 personnel in a critical 3rd down situation. The Y's responsibility on this play is to arc release out of the backfield in order to widen out his defender and create more space for pullers and quarterback to run through. If we feel that 12 personnel does not put our best 11 on the field to execute this concept, we can accomplish the same feat out of 11 personnel. By replacing the play side tight end with a slot receiver and running this play out of Deuce Up, we force the defense to spread out and lighten their box. We are just doing it pre-snap now instead of how Clemson did it with the Y post-snap.

This modification would result in us losing our pre-snap ambiguity as the formation will no longer be mirrored. If this is the adjustment that we choose, we must be sure to run various other concepts out of the same formation.

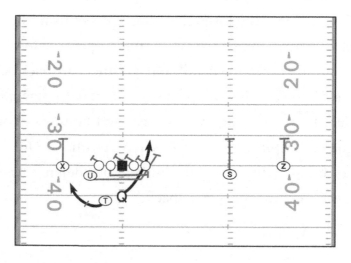

*Fake Toss QB Counter out of 11 Personnel GW Deuce Up*

# +35 YARD SCORING PASSES

# 5
## FOUR VERTS
### 2018 CFP CHAMPIONSHIP

### ALABAMA CRIMSON TIDE VS.
### GEORGIA BULLDOGS

**— CHAMPION —**

**ALABAMA CRIMSON TIDE**

# FOUR VERTS

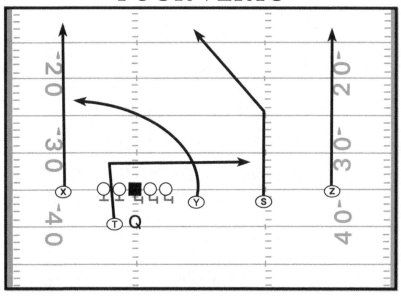

| POSITION | ALIGNMENT | ASSIGNMENT | COACHING NOTE |
|---|---|---|---|
| Q | GUN | DBP | MOFO READ - POST; MOFC READ - FADE TO DEEP OVER; HOT - FADE; CHECK DOWN - T |
| T | SPLIT OG/OT; TOES TO HEELS | FIELD CHECK DOWN | BLITZ PICK UP 1ST REPSONSIBILITY, NO BLITZ = CHECK DOWN |
| X | BOUND. TOP #s | FADE | HOLD BOTTOM #s & FADE TO SL W/ BALL, CATCH OVER O.S. SHOULDER W/ HIGH HANDS |
| Z | FIELD TOP #s | FADE | HOLD BOTTOM #s & FADE TO SL W/ BALL, CATCH OVER O.S. SHOULDER W/ HIGH HANDS |
| S | HASH +1 | 10-YD POST | BIG POST, DO NOT CROSS MOF, NEED TO KEEP DEEP SAFETIES IN CONFLICT |
| Y | EOL +2 | DEEP OVER | 12-15 YDS; ZONE = FIND SOFT SPOT, MAN = SPRINT TO SIDELINE |
| OL | BASE | 51 | PS = LT; 5-MAN PASS PRO; HALF SLIDE RT |

## FORMATION: GW TRIPS
## PERSONNEL: 11
## MOTION: N/A

## SCHEME:

You may want to skip this one, Georgia fans – the infamous 2$^{nd}$ & 26. This four verticals concept by Alabama is a brilliant shot-taking scheme as it includes beaters for multiple coverages. Georgia implements a split-field coverage scheme that has become almost standard throughout college football, and even some high school football as well.

While split-field coverage was designed in response to modern offenses' increased passing attacks, we must not let it deter us from taking shots downfield with four verticals concepts. Despite its popularity, split-field coverage is complicated and difficult for many secondaries to execute at a high level. This leads to many blown coverages, including the one featured on this play, which resulted in the game-winning touchdown of the 2018 CFP National Championship game. This four verticals concept is a proven answer for any 2-high safety coverage as it has a built-in beater for both Cover 2 and Cover 4. It will serve us well on any of our favorite shot-taking downs & distances as long as we can protect long enough with a 5-man protection.

## PRE-SNAP:

Georgia shows a 2-high safety shell, prompting Alabama's quarterback to believe he will see 1 of 2 coverages: Cover 2 or Cover 4. His pre-snap Cover 2 read is the post. Since Cover 2 contains 2 safeties, each responsible for a deep half of the field, the middle of the field is the weak spot in the zone.

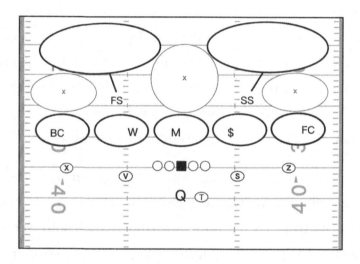

*Cover 2 vs. Doubles*

Contrary to Cover 2, Cover 4 divides the deep part of the field into 4 zones, usually manned by both corners and both safeties. The pre-snap Cover 4 read for Bama's quarterback is the deep over. The deep 1/4 corner should follow the boundary fade, vacating the 15–20-yard zone near the boundary sideline – flat defenders always struggle to get enough depth to cover this throw.

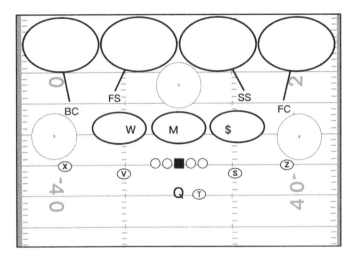

*Cover 4 vs. Doubles*

## POST-SNAP:

As the ball is snapped, Alabama sees neither Cover 4 nor Cover 2, but a combination of both, known as Cover 6 (4 + 2 = 6). Cover 6 features Cover 4 to one side of the field and Cover 2 to the other. This is the essence of split-field coverage. One coverage is executed by the defenders aligned to the boundary, while another coverage is implemented by the defenders aligned to the field. In Cover 6, almost always, the Cover 4 side is to the field and the Cover 2 side is to the boundary.

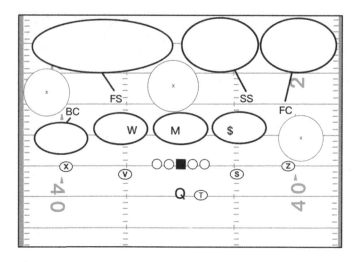

*Cover 6 vs. Doubles*

Georgia's boundary safety takes off towards the deep boundary half, while the field safety remains on the hash. The Bulldogs are actually in the best possible call to stop Alabama's version of 4 verts. The deep 1/2 safety should be playing over the top of the X. The field corner and field safety each have their respective deep routes. And the Cover 2 corner should carry the vertical by X until Y enters his zone, then he drives on Y. The breakdown occurs with the boundary safety. Seeing the vertical release by #3 strong, he begins to drift back onto the hash to protect the middle of the field. By abandoning his Cover 2 landmark, he is out of position to make a play on #1 weak in the end zone.

Despite the lapse in coverage, Alabama still needed near perfect execution on the throw and catch to complete this championship-winning touchdown. When throwing a deep fade down the sideline, we are aiming for 40x4 – 40 yards down the field and 4 yards from the sideline. That is the optimal location to hit our receiver in stride while also keeping the ball away from the safety and allowing the receiver space to work with after the catch. This is an extremely difficult throw to make; even the best offenses complete only about 25% of them on average. This ball was snapped at the 41-yard line and caught in stride at the 1-yard line, 4 yards from the sideline – a perfect throw and catch.

## ADJUSTMENTS:

On the off chance that a Cover 6 defense is able to consistently stifle this 4 verticals concept, we can adjust the inside routes to include a Cover 6 beater as well. Converting #2 strong's route to a seam vertical right up the hash will hold the field Cover 4 safety. #3 strong will then run the deep post to attack the weak, middle of the field zone. This puts the boundary Cover 2 safety in conflict as he must choose between the vertical by #1 weak and the post by #3 strong.

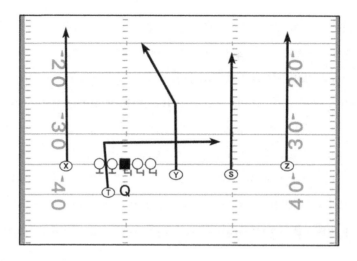

*4 Verts Adjustment — Cover 6 Beater*

However, Alabama's original concept is not limited to shredding 2-high coverage schemes. It can be just as lethal versus single-high looks such as Cover 1 and Cover 3. Against these schemes, our target route is going to be the deep over by #3 strong. Both fades and the post route should be picked up by each of the deep 1/3 defenders (or followed by their man defenders in Cover 1). In order to cover the deep over, the boundary flat defender must sink at least 15 yards downfield – highly unlikely.

Since the deep over throw is slower-developing than the others, we should consider two more potential adjustments: altering personnel and protection. In Alabama's scheme, #3 strong is a tight end. If we are facing a heavy dose of Cover 3, it may be in our best interest to execute this concept out of 10 personnel so that #3 strong can hit that 15–20-yard landmark faster than a tight end would. We also need to consider converting the protection scheme from a 5-man half slide to a 6-man half slide, adding the back in the protection. This will provide the quarterback the extra time needed for this long route concept to develop.

# 6

## PAP SWITCH FOLLOW

### 2020 ACC CHAMPIONSHIP

### CLEMSON TIGERS VS. NOTRE DAME FIGHTING IRISH

— CHAMPION —

**CLEMSON TIGERS**

# PAP SWITCH FOLLOW

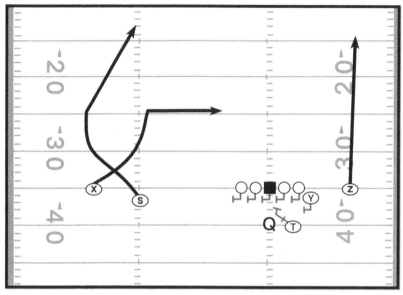

| POSITION | ALIGNMENT | ASSIGNMENT | COACHING NOTE |
|---|---|---|---|
| Q | GUN | PAP | 1ST READ - BOUNDARY FADE; 2ND READ - SKINNY POST; 3RD READ - DIG |
| T | SPLIT OG/OT; 1 YD BEHIND QB | PLAY ACTION FAKE; PASS PRO | PROTECT AWAY FROM SLIDE, PS D-GAP |
| X | DIV. HASH & #s | SWITCH RELEASE; 10-YD DIG | CROSS 1ST ON THE SWICH RELEASE; GET TO THE HASH BEFORE BREAKING ON DIG |
| Z | BOUND. BOT. #s | FADE | STAY ON THE #s UNTIL THE BALL TAKES YOU OFF |
| S | FIELD HASH | SWITCH RELEASE; 10-YD POST | CROSS 2ND ON SWITCH RELEASE; DIV. HASH & #s BEFORE BREAKING ON POST; SKINNY POST |
| Y | I.S./O.S.; 2 YDS BEHIND OT | SLIDE LT PASS PRO | PROTECT PS C-GAP |
| OL | BASE | 78 | PS = RT; 7-MAN PASS PRO; FULL SLIDE LT, NOBODY LOCK |

**FORMATION: GW DEUCE UP**
**PERSONNEL: 11**
**MOTION: N/A**

## SCHEME:

This is an excellent shot to take at the start of a drive as long as we set it up first. Notice how this formation is very similar to Georgia's inside zone scheme (prior to the SAC motion). In that breakdown, we examined the purpose of running inside zone on base downs; now we will discuss a major benefit of doing so.

Prior to this explosive play, Clemson had been consistently hitting inside zone for positive yardage on base downs. This play action concept is designed to mimic inside zone left, as everybody in protection, including the TE, slide protects to the field. We can really set this play up nicely by successfully executing Georgia's inside zone scheme with and without the SAC motion. The comparable formations will manipulate the defense into a run-stopping call, ill-prepared to cover this play action pass concept.

Follow is a common pass concept containing a post route on the outside and dig route on the inside. It is designed to beat single-high coverages such as Cover 1 and Cover 3 because it puts the post safety in conflict. The safety must choose between staying on top of the post and driving on the dig.

Since both the tight end and the running back remain in pass protection, the linebackers are ultimately responsible for cutting off the throw to the dig. That is why the setup of this play is so crucial. Linebackers are run defenders first and pass defenders second. Clemson's prior inside zone success lures Notre Dame's linebackers up to the line of scrimmage as the quarterback and running back engage in the play action fake. The deceived linebackers imply to the post safety that they will be ill-positioned to cut the dig, so he feels the need to drive on it. As soon as the post safety shows the slightest forward movement, we hit the post over the top for a touchdown. If he remains in his deep zone and covers the post, we throw the dig over the linebackers' heads.

PRE-SNAP:

Notre Dame's pre-snap look indicates a 4-3 under front, accompanied by Cover 1 on the back end. Versus man coverage, our quarterback's first read is the fade by the Z receiver since that is the quickest developing route. The switch follow concept needs time to develop so we must have a more immediate read in the meantime. If the Z wins right off the line of scrimmage, we will abandon the field concept and take our shot in the boundary. The key coaching note for the quarterback when throwing a quick vertical into the boundary versus Cover 1 is to read the post safety prior to taking the shot. The quarterback's eye progression needs to be receiver release, post safety, throwing target. If we throw that vertical into the boundary without checking the safety first, he may float over the top and pick it off.

## POST-SNAP:

Clemson's Z receiver fails to win off the line, so the quarterback's eyes shift to the follow concept. The play action concept works to perfection on this play. By the time Clemson's quarterback finishes his 3-step drop, all three of Notre Dame's second level defenders are within 2 yards of the line of scrimmage. The X receiver has plenty of room to attack that 10–12-yard zone and conflict the post safety.

The S runs behind the X on the switch release and the Notre Dame DBs do not switch who they are guarding; they each stick with their original man. The coverage breakdown occurs exactly where it is targeted, the post. Due to the length of time that Clemson's quarterback stares down the boundary fade, the post safety commits to bracketing the Z receiver. By doing so, he abandons his middle of the field zone, leading to an easy pitch and catch to the S for a 67-yard score.

## ADJUSTMENTS:

This is an excellent single-high safety beater, but it can easily be converted into a 2-high beater if that is the style of defense we more commonly face. This 1-high beater aims to lure the post safety into opening up the middle of the field. Since the middle of the field is already open versus a 2-high shell, we need to find a way to occupy both deep 1/2 safeties while simultaneously attacking the open middle of the field zone. To do this, we only need to slightly adjust the routes of our X and S receivers. Instead of breaking on a post, the S will continue on his vertical path, drifting towards the top of the numbers. The X will simply break on post at 10 yards rather than a dig. This will send 3 vertical routes into the 2 safeties' deep 1/2 zones.

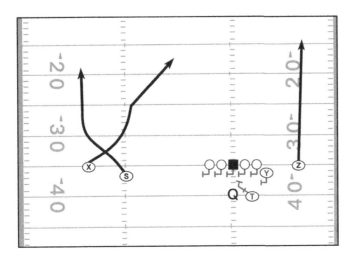

*PAP Switch Follow Adjustment — Middle of the Field Open Beater*

# 7
## VERT/DIG
### 2022 CFP CHAMPIONSHIP
### GEORGIA BULLDOGS VS. ALABAMA CRIMSON TIDE

**— CHAMPION —**
**GEORGIA BULLDOGS**

# VERT/DIG

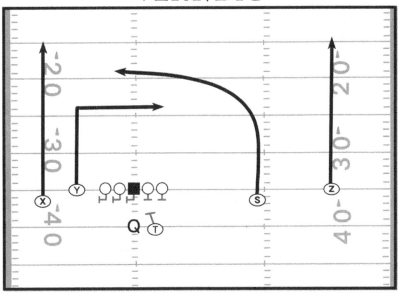

| POSITION | ALIGNMENT | ASSIGNMENT | COACHING NOTE |
|---|---|---|---|
| Q | GUN | DBP | BOUNDARY FADE IS HOT; TAKE SHOT TO O.S. W/ 1-ON-1 COVERAGE |
| T | SPLIT OG/OT; EVEN WITH QB | PASS PRO | PROTECT MAN SIDE |
| X | BOUNDARY BOTTOM #s | FADE | OFF LOS; STAY ON BOT. #s UNTIL BALL TAKES YOU OFF |
| Z | FIELD TOP #s | FADE | STAY ON THE TOP OF #s UNTIL THE BALL TAKES YOU OFF |
| S | FIELD HASH | SPEED DIG | BREAK AT 10 YDS, ROUND TO 15 |
| Y | DIV. HASH AND #s; ON LOS | 11-YD DIG | SQUARE CUT DIG |
| OL | BASE | 60 | PS = RT; 6-MAN PASS PRO; HALF SLIDE LT |

**FORMATION: GS DOUBLES INVERT**
**PERSONNEL:** 11
**MOTION: N/A**

SCHEME:

Alright Georgia fans, you can look again. The Bulldogs now find themselves on the opposite end of a perfect 40x4 ball.

Although football is the ultimate team sport, each play contains 11 1-on-1 matchups. Winning these 1-on-1 matchups is crucial to our ability to create explosive plays and score points. As our level of football increases, it becomes increasingly difficult to scheme players open. We must instead rely on our players' abilities to beat the man in front of them. Our goal, then, is to draw up schemes that put our players in the best positions to win their 1-on-1 matchups.

Georgia does an excellent job demonstrating this concept for a 40-yard, go-ahead touchdown in the fourth quarter of the CFP Championship. In this simple vertical/dig concept, the key component is the dig by #2 strong. The 10–15-yard speed cut of the route is deep enough to demand attention from both a 1-high and 2-high shell, assuring that #1 strong will be 1-on-1 with the field corner.

This is a great call to either take a shot on 1st down or convert on a critical 3rd & long. Either the safeties will respect the deep dig, leaving their corner on an island, or they will stay over the top. In which case, we hit the deep dig for a 1$^{st}$ down. Find that DB that the defense is trying to hide and force him to win a 1-on-1 matchup with your best receiver.

PRE-SNAP:

Alabama only plays 2 down defensive linemen – an indication that they are playing the pass all the way. With 2 walked up linebackers, they show blitz. The pre-snap hot read on this play is the boundary vertical since it is the quickest developing route. However, Georgia's quarterback knows that they have a 6-man protection dialed up. So, he does not need to worry about getting the ball out quickly in the event that both linebackers blitz. With 2 D-linemen and 2 blitzers, Georgia still has a 6-4 advantage against the pass rush.

It's extremely important for our quarterback to understand the pass protection, as well as the strength and direction of potential pressure from the defense. This knowledge will allow him to remain calm in the pocket and maximize his ability to make sound decisions. Understanding they have a 6-4 protection advantage, Georgia's quarterback knows he will have the luxury of keeping his eyes down field long enough to take a shot at the end zone.

POST-SNAP:

The Tide end up bringing just 3 on the pass rush. Georgia's O-line capitalizes on this by providing their quarterback with ample time to find the hole in Bama's secondary. The coverage scheme that the Tide are running on this play has been a staple in Saban-led defenses for years. It's called match quarters.

Match quarters is a pattern matching defense based on Cover 4. Pattern matching is a coverage scheme that allows the offense's route concepts to dictate the coverage that the defense runs. Simply put, it starts out as a zone defense but turns into man once the receiver's route patterns have distributed. Each coverage defender must abide by position-specific pattern matching rules. The rules for the corners are: if #1 is out or vertical, he's mine; if 1 is underneath, I let him go and squeeze to the next vertical threat. The safeties' rules are determined by the #2 receiver: if #2 is vertical, he's mine; if he's out or underneath, I bracket #1.

Against Georgia's Vert/Dig concept, both corners match their #1 receivers vertically, and both safeties match their #2 receivers vertically. The definition of a vertical route is subjective, and usually determined by the defensive coordinator's preference. The general principle, however, is anything over 5 yards is a vertical route. This rule requires both safeties to commit to the digs, leaving the corners on an island against the deep ball. The success of this play, however, comes down to the receivers being able to win their 1-on-1 matchups. A perfect 40x4 ball to #1 strong, and the

Bulldogs reclaim the 4<sup>th</sup> quarter lead from their conference foe.

## ADJUSTMENTS:

Seeing that match quarters coverage is a more advanced coverage scheme, we may not see it throughout all levels of football. Instead, we are more likely to encounter true zone coverages such as Cover 4, Cover 2 and Cover 3. While this route concept will do just fine against those coverages, we can still tailor it to better suit our needs.

This original concept is designed to beat match coverage as it requires the deep safeties to drive on the digs. In a true zone scheme, deep safeties will not drive on intermediate routes; they must be deeper than the deepest. Instead, the linebackers are responsible for sinking underneath intermediate routes. Therefore, if we switch #2 strong's route from a deep dig to a post, that will better attack the weaknesses of true zone coverages as it will creep into the deep middle of the field and occupy any deep safeties. With the safeties being occupied by this deep post, we assure that the corners will remain on an island with our outside receivers.

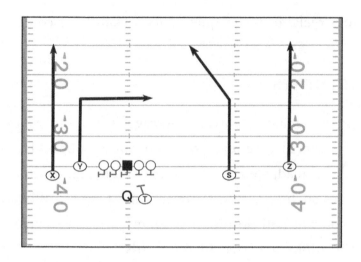

*Vert/Dig Adjustment — True Zone Coverage Beater*

# 8

## PAP SLOT DEEP OVER

### 2021 CFP CHAMPIONSHIP

### ALABAMA CRIMSON TIDE VS. THE OHIO STATE BUCKEYES

**— CHAMPION —**

**ALABAMA CRIMSON TIDE**

# PAP SLOT DEEP OVER

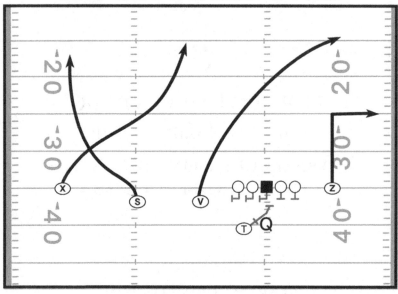

| POSITION | ALIGNMENT | ASSIGNMENT | COACHING NOTE |
|---|---|---|---|
| Q | GUN | PAP | MOFO READ - SWITCH VERTICAL CONCEPT; MOFC READ - POST SAFETY |
| T | SPLIT OG/OT; EVEN WITH QB | PLAY ACTION FAKE; PASS PRO | PROTECT MAN SIDE |
| X | FIELD TOP #s | SWITCH RELEASE; MOF VERTICAL | CROSS 1ST ON SWITCH RELEASE; MOFC: PULL EYES OF POST SAFETY |
| Z | BOUNDARY TOP #s | 10-YD OUT | NEED TO SELL THIS ROUTE TO GET THE CB TO BITE |
| S | FIELD HASH | SWITCH RELEASE; SL VERTICAL | CROSS 2ND ON SWITCH RELEASE; LANDMARK = TOP #s |
| V | MOF | DEEP OVER | CROSS UNDER SAM LB AND OVER MIKE LB; CROSS HASH AT 15 YDS, WORK UP TO 20 |
| OL | BASE | 60 | PS = RT; 6-MAN PASS PRO HALF SLIDE LT |

**FORMATION: GS TRIPS**
**PERSONNEL: 10**
**MOTION: N/A**

SCHEME:

Similar to many of our other deep shots in this chapter, this is a great call on base downs and $3^{rd}$ & long. However, more important than the situational down and distance for this call, is catching our opponent in a single-high safety look. This deep over concept is an absolute nightmare for Cover 1 and Cover 3 defenses.

Versus Cover 1, we put the post safety in conflict as he must choose between helping on the deep over by #3 strong and helping on the switch vertical by #1 strong. Both of these routes are designed to require post safety help in order to be properly defended. Requiring a man coverage defender to follow a receiver across the width of the field is an extremely tall order. This is especially true when that receiver is aligned in the slot, as their defensive counterparts – linebackers and safeties – are generally slower than they are. These defenders will require over-the-top help to avoid being burned on a deep over route.

While #1 strong – being guarded by a corner – may not have the same speed advantage as #3 strong, the switch release into his vertical route is likely to create just enough separation, allowing him to gain a step on his man defender. Now that both #1 strong and #3 strong are in advantageous positions, we read the post safety and hit whichever route he chooses not to help.

Whereas the post safety is our defender in conflict versus Cover 1, against Cover 3, our defender in conflict will be the boundary corner. He must choose between the out route by #1 weak and the deep over by #3 strong. Our objective is to entice the deep 1/3 corner to drive on the out route, believing he has no vertical threats in his zone, so that we may hit the deep over behind him for an explosive completion.

PRE-SNAP:

True 10 personnel sets have become more of a rarity in today's college football. If we have a dominant O-line that can run the ball effectively without tight end or full back assistance, then 10 personnel is the way to go. It offers an enormous advantage in the pass game while not sacrificing production in the run game. Fortunately for Alabama, this is exactly the manner in which their 2020 squad was constructed.

Ohio State shows single-high, zone coverage pre-snap. They play a 4-down front with both linebackers in the box, giving them a 6-5 numbers advantage in the run game. Alabama's ability to move the chains through their 10-personnel ground attack forces Ohio State to commit extra defenders to stopping the run even out of a pass-heavy formation.

POST-SNAP:

The Buckeyes play true Cover 3 with a slight adjustment. True Cover 3 consists of 3 deep zones and 4 underneath zones.

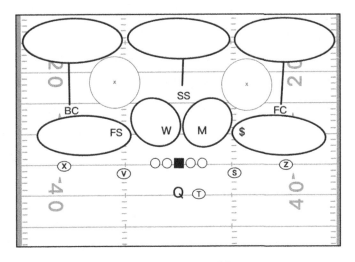

*True Cover 3 vs. Doubles*

It is common practice for many defenses to have their corner on the backside of 3x1 play man coverage on the wide out to the single receiver side. This is exactly what Ohio State does with their boundary corner. The deep over concept aims to beat Cover 3 by sneaking the over route behind the deep 1/3 corner from the opposite side of the field. With Ohio State's Cover 3 adjustment, the boundary corner is occupied by the out route and the deep over slips into the boundary deep 1/3 with ease.

The technique used by #3 strong to run the deep over route is vital. He must run under the Sam linebacker (or nickel) and over the Mike linebacker. If he runs over the Sam, he runs the risk of being re-routed into the safety. And if he runs under the Mike, he will not reach his proper route depth without being detected by the boundary corner.

In addition to route precision, another key component of this successful play is the play action. Already respecting the run threat with a numbers advantage in the box, Ohio State's linebackers must wait until they are certain it is a pass until they can sink to their coverage zones. The play action freezes the second level defenders just long enough to allows #3 strong to get into his route and work to his proper depth without being re-routed.

ADJUSTMENTS:

This design was specifically drawn up to attack defenses that adjust their Cover 3 scheme by playing man on the back side. However, in true Cover 3, some corners are extremely disciplined and will not bite on the out by #1 weak. If we are facing a true Cover 3 defense in which the back side corner holds deep 1/3 responsibility, we can increase our chances of putting him in conflict by running a fade route with #1 weak. The deep 1/3 corner will stay on top of #1 weak's vertical and we will be able to hit the over route on top of the boundary flat defender. In order to do this, the depth of the over route should be altered from the 18-22 yard range to the 12-15 yard range to assure that the corner cannot drive on the route and make a play on the ball.

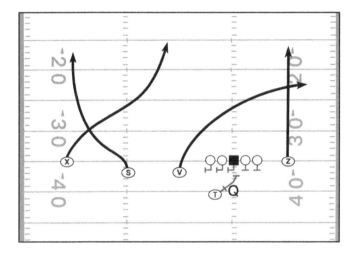

*PAP Slot Deep Over Adjustment — True Cover 3 Beater*

# 9
## LEVELS
2021 SEC CHAMPIONSHIP

ALABAMA CRIMSON TIDE VS.
GEORGIA BULLDOGS


**— CHAMPION —**
**ALABAMA CRIMSON TIDE**

# LEVELS

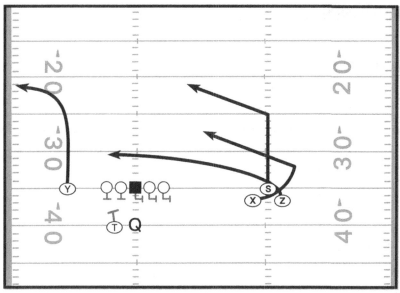

| POSITION | ALIGNMENT | ASSIGNMENT | COACHING NOTE |
|----------|-----------|------------|---------------|
| Q | GUN | DBP | 1ST READ - POST, 2ND READ - SLANT, 3RD READ - UNDER |
| T | SPLIT OG/OT; EVEN WITH QB | PASS PRO | PROTECT MAN SIDE |
| X | HASH -1; OFF LOS | SLANT | RELEASE 3RD OUT OF BUNCH; SQUARE UP DB BEFORE BREAKING IN |
| Z | HASH +1; OFF LOS | UNDER | RELEASE 2ND OUT OF BUNCH; 3 YDS ON UNDER ROUTE |
| S | HASH; BUNCH POINT; ON LOS | 10-YD BANG POST | RELEASE 1ST OUT OF BUNCH; LOOK FOR BALL IMMEDIATELY AFTER BREAKING ON POST |
| Y | BOUND. TOP #s | SPEED OUT | BREAK AT 10 YDS, ROUND TO 15 |
| OL | BASE | 61 | PS = LT; 6-MAN PASS PRO; HALF SLIDE RT |

**FORMATION: GW TRIPS BUNCH**
**PERSONNEL: 11**
**MOTION: N/A**

SCHEME:

One of our jobs as offensive coordinators is to create as much confusion as possible for the defense, while simultaneously keeping our concepts as simple as possible for our offense. Bunch sets are a great way to generate defensive confusion and blown coverages, leading to explosive plays.

This is a great 3$^{rd}$ down call because it is a beater for several extremely common 3$^{rd}$ down coverages: fire zones, man to man, and Tampa 2. Fire zones and man coverage are most commonly run on 3$^{rd}$ down because they accompany blitzes. Defensive coordinators love to blitz on 3$^{rd}$ down to prevent the quarterback from being able to make an accurate decision and throw. Since Georgia's defense runs a fire zone on this play, we will discuss them in our post-snap breakdown. The following paragraphs will analyze this concepts' ability to attack man to man and Tampa 2.

A common man coverage response to a bunch set is to place the corner on the point man, accompanied by 2 defenders on either side of him. The corner jams the point man while the 2 side defenders play banjo technique over the #1 and #3 receivers. Banjo technique means that the defense has 2 defenders guarding 2 offenders. The outside banjo defender will take the first outside route and the inside banjo defender will take the first inside route. If both routes go outside then the inside defender will take the second outside route. And if both routes go inside then the outside defender will take the second inside route.

By this rule, the inside banjo defender should be taking the Z, and the outside banjo defender should be taking the S. As the inside defender follows the Z on the underneath route, that vacates the zone in the shallow middle of the field. The S already has inside leverage on the outside defender, so he should have no issues winning on the inside as he breaks back towards the vacated middle of the field zone. With the S having at least 1 step on his man defender, it will result in an easy pitch and catch 1$^{st}$ down for the offense.

One of the more commonly ran true zone coverage on 3$^{rd}$ down is Tampa 2. This coverage allows the Cover 2 corners to sink underneath and potentially cut off deep outs, while also closing off the middle of the field with a deep runner. Tampa 2 involves base Cover 2 rules, with a middle of the field runner – usually the Mike linebacker – to take away the normally-vacated middle of the field zone. Alabama's levels concept is a Tampa 2 beater because it puts multiple defenders in conflict: the middle of the field player and the boundary corner. The middle of the field defender must choose between the X's high route and the S's low route that both cross into his zone.

If neither of those routes are open, we then read the boundary corner. He must choose between the deep out by #1 weak and the underneath route by #1 strong that eventually enters his zone. Depending on the down and distance, we may be able to hit that shallow cross for a 1st down.

Since our quarterback must read the zone defenders in conflict, the routes take slightly longer to open up than they do versus man coverage. We must have sound protection to successfully use this play to attack zone coverage. If we do not have the ability to protect long enough to allow these routes to develop versus zone, then this play should be limited to beating match (fire zone) and man coverages.

PRE-SNAP:

Georgia's secondary shows a pre-snap 2-high shell, a pre-snap victory for Alabama. As previously discussed, 2-high coverages are vulnerable in the middle of the field. This route concept sends 2 receivers to the middle of the field at different levels, so even if Georgia did have a middle of the field player, that defender would be in conflict and would need to choose between the high route and the low route.

Alabama comes out in a Trips Bunch set to the field. Bunches are extremely difficult on coverage defenders because they require abundant and accurate communication to successfully defend. Alabama's bunch formation creates a coverage breakdown in Georgia's secondary, leading to this explosive touchdown.

POST-SNAP:

Georgia brings a 5-man pressure, leaving 6 defenders in coverage on the back end. This defensive scheme is often referred to as a fire zone. Fire zones generally play zone coverage behind the blitz with their 6 coverage defenders – 3 deep and 3 underneath. However, in short yardage situations, like this 3$^{rd}$ & 2, it is common practice to play match coverage behind the 5-man blitz.

Fire zone matching rules are very similar to the match quarter rules that we broke down earlier in this chapter. There is a defender (usually a corner) on each side of the ball to match the #1 receiver, and a defender on each side of the ball to match #2 – same technique as match quarters. Then there is a post player. The 6$^{th}$ coverage defender is the final #3 player. His responsibility is to match whichever route becomes the #3 receiver after the routes have distributed. In other words, he matches the most inside route. On this play, it's the underneath route by the Z. Generally, the non-blitzing linebacker is the final #3 player in a fire zone matching scheme. But on this play, Georgia blitzes both of their linebackers. In these instances, the final #3 player is the non-post safety.

This scheme by Alabama is a fire zone beater due to the bunch set. When a defense is blitzing, they expect that the ball is going to be out of the quarterback's hands quickly because they trust their blitz to hit home. This is why we often see man coverage played behind blitzes. Versus a bunch set, many fire zone match coverages will check to a true 3 deep, 3 underneath fire zone so that they can properly view the route distribution and will not get picked by crossing routes and switch releases.

This coverage check is not properly communicated throughout Georgia's secondary as half of them play match coverage while the other half play true 3 deep, 3 underneath. This causes a gaping hole to open up in the middle of the field, and nobody follows the X on the bang post, resulting in the 69-yard score.

ADJUSTMENTS:

While Alabama executes this concept out of 11 personnel, it may be beneficial to many of us to run it out of 10 personnel. All 3 receivers in the bunch need to be speed players in order to increase the speed at which the defenders must communicate. So, Alabama places their tight end at #1 weak to run a deep out. One of the reasons that the X had so much running room after the catch was due to the tight end's ability to pull his coverage defender all the way to the sideline with his route. A lesser pass-catching threat of a tight end would not have had the same effect on the defense, and the corner may have been in position to make the tackle, resulting in just a 1$^{st}$ down instead of a touchdown. Each route in this levels concept is vital in the way that it manipulates the defense. We need to be prepared to adjust our personnel properly in order to execute this scheme and yield the most positive results.

# 10

## SLANT/ANGLE

### 2017 BIG 12 CHAMPIONSHIP

### OKLAHOMA SOONERS VS. TCU HORNED FROGS

**— CHAMPION —**

**OKLAHOMA SOONERS**

# SLANT/ANGLE

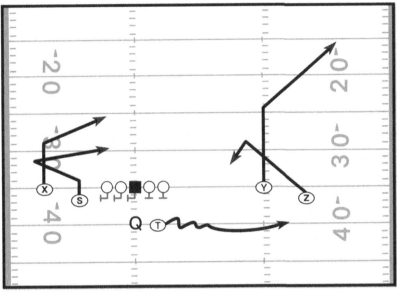

| POSITION | ALIGNMENT | ASSIGNMENT | COACHING NOTE |
|----------|-----------|------------|---------------|
| Q | GUN | DBP | SNAP BALL WHEN T IS MOF; S IS PRIMARY RECEIVER |
| T | SPLIT OG/OT; 1 YD BEHIND QB | ROPE MOTION; SWING ROUTE | MAINTAIN ROUTE 5 YDS DEEP IN BACKFIELD |
| X | BOUND. BOT. #s | 5-STEP SLANT | DEPTH DETERMINED BY YARDAGE INSTEAD OF STEPS; STEP COUNT HELPS WITH QB/WR TIMING |
| Z | DIV. HASH & #s; OFF LOS | 6-YD SNAG | MOTOR DOWN AFTER CROSSING HASH, FIND OPEN SPOT IN ZONE |
| S | DIV. EOL & #s | ANGLE | REVERSE PIVOT & OPEN TO QB, OR SPEED TURN BACK INSIDE (COACH/PLAYER PREFERENCE) |
| Y | FIELD HASH; ON LOS | 10-YD CORNER | 2-HIGH SAFETIES = FLATTEN TOWARDS SL; 1-HIGH SAFETY = SKINNY ANGLE TO PYLON |
| OL | BASE | 50 | PS = RT; 5-MAN PASS PRO; HALF SLIDE LT |

## FORMATION: GS DOUBLES INVERT
## PERSONNEL: 11
## MOTION: TIF ROPE

### SCHEME:

The success of this play will depend largely on our ability to correctly set it up and create the ideal mismatch. This is a solid base down call – particularly on 1st down. Since most offensive coordinators on 1st down are trying to get to 2nd and short or 2nd & medium, they often run concepts like RB bubble or slant/flat because they are easy completions that often go for positive yards. Fortunately, this scheme provides several options that will all play a role in creating the perfect mismatch.

Our goal is to hit the S on the angle route, providing him with plenty of open space in the middle of the field to turn this short completion into an explosive play. To do this, we need to throw a few bubble screens to the back. This will cause the linebackers to flow that direction when they recognize the TIF motion.

A staple in many offensive playbooks is the slant/flat concept. A slant route by #1 and a flat route by #2. By hitting a couple of flat routes out of this formation we entice the flat defender to jump that route the next time he encounters it. After successfully executing a few bubble screens and flat routes, this slant/angle concept will be an excellent changeup that will ambush any defense that anticipates one of our previous 1$^{st}$ down plays.

PRE-SNAP:

By setting the tight end to the field, and 2 speed receivers to the boundary, Oklahoma obtains their desired mismatch. The defensive personnel that the Horned Frogs have on the field is conducive to countering 11 personnel sets, but not the way Oklahoma runs them.

TCU is playing with a 3 down front and a bandit defender. The term, bandit, is not a universal term, but it is commonly used to refer to the overhang defender that is a defensive end/linebacker hybrid. The bandit is usually the boundary flat defender in zone coverage and the hot of #2 player in fire zone match coverage. He almost always aligns to the boundary so that if he does need to cover, he only has to do so with a small amount of space. A tight end versus a bandit in coverage is a fairly even matchup. A bandit versus a slot receiver, on the other hand, advantage offense. Since one of our objective is to create and exploit mismatches in order to win 1-on-1 matchups, aligning your slot receiver to the boundary and your tight end to the field accomplishes exactly that.

POST-SNAP:

A quick, post-snap safety rotation reveals that the Horned Frogs will not stay in their 2-high shell. The field safety rotates down strong side and the boundary safety rotates back into the post – it is drop 8 Cover 3. Drop 8 Cover 3 means that the defense has 8 defenders in coverage – 3 deep and 5 underneath. A coverage scheme with that many underneath defenders versus a shallow route concept like this one should leave the quarterback with nowhere to throw the ball. However, the previously-utilized field concept of this play is used perfectly to create the optimal boundary mismatch, resulting in a 55-yard touchdown.

The field corner must squeeze to the corner route by the tight end. The TIF rope motion causes the Sam linebacker and the strong safety to both commit to the bubble; this frees up the snag route by 1 strong. Seeing the snag route open, the Mike linebacker leaves his zone to push to the open receiver; this vacates the shallow middle of the field. To the boundary, the Will linebacker must run with the slant by #1 weak since the Mike is not there for the exchange; this creates an even larger gap in the shallow middle of the field. This results in our fastest receiver, #2 weak, being matched up in space with their slowest coverage defender, the bandit. Again, it's another easy pitch and catch that explodes for a touchdown because we were able to manipulate and exploit a mismatch.

## ADJUSTMENTS:

The most important part of this play is creating the mismatch that will yield the best result. If our S receiver is not typically the best playmaker, it is okay to manipulate the alignments to give ourselves the look that we want. Let's say our X gives us the best matchup; we can design this play to have the X lined up at #2 weak and the S at #1 weak. We should not be afraid of adjusting the norms of our playbook if it will create a winning matchup for us. At the end of the day, the players' job is to make plays; our job is to put them in the right position to do so.

# 11

## DOUBLE SLUGGO
### 2019 PAC 12 CHAMPIONSHIP
### OREGON DUCKS VS. UTAH UTES


**— CHAMPION —**
**OREGON DUCKS**

# DOUBLE SLUGGO

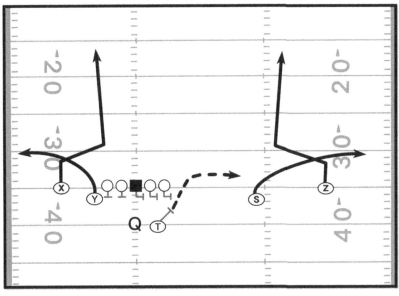

| POSITION | ALIGNMENT | ASSIGNMENT | COACHING NOTE |
|----------|-----------|------------|---------------|
| Q | GUN | DBP | MAN READ - THROW OVER THE TOP; ZONE READ - THROW INTO SEAM; PUMP FAKE SLANT |
| T | SPLIT OG/OT; EVEN WITH QB | PASS PRO 1ST; CHECK DOWN 2ND | RELEASE INTO CHECK DOWN AS SOON AS THERE IS NO IMMEDIATE PASS RUSH THREAT |
| X | BOUND. TOP #s | SLUGGO | BREAK ON SLANT ON 5TH STEP, BREAK ON GO ON 3RD STEP AFTER SLANT BREAK; DRIFT O.S. OF HASH |
| Z | FIELD TOP #s | SLUGGO | BREAK ON SLANT ON 5TH STEP, BREAK ON GO ON 3RD STEP AFTER SLANT BREAK; DRIFT O.S. OF HASH |
| S | FIELD HASH -1 | SPEED OUT | AIM FOR SL AT 5 YDS |
| Y | I.S./O.S.; 1 YD BEHIND OT | SPEED OUT | AIM FOR SL AT 5 YDS |
| OL | BASE | 61 | PS = LT; 6-MAN PASS PRO; HALF SLIDE RT |

## FORMATION: GS DEUCE UP
## PERSONNEL: 11
## MOTION: N/A

### SCHEME:

Similar to our previous double move concept, this play must also be set up through proper execution of several slant/flat route combinations. When an offense is having success completing simple slant routes, the defense is forced to play man coverage in an attempt to take that route away with inside leverage. This works out perfectly for us because the sluggo concept is a man killer. As soon as we recognize man, we can hit this deadly double move for an explosive 6 points.

This is an effective play on any down, but there are a couple of factors to consider in order to increase our chances of running it against the correct coverage. Remember, man coverage is a heavy 3rd down call for defenses because they will often blitz in those situations. Also, the down and distance on which we run this play should be consistent with the down and distance on which we run our standard slant/flat concept. If we've been executing slant/flat on base downs, and the defense is now playing man coverage on base downs, then we will have a higher chance of success with this concept on a base down. Studying our opponents' tendencies is key to dialing up the perfect play at the perfect time.

## PRE-SNAP:

The pre-snap look shown by Utah's secondary is 1-high. This should indicate to the quarterback that we are going to get either Cover 1 or Cover 3 – both middle of the field closed defenses. Utah's DBs show man coverage, aligning directly over their offensive counterparts, some indicating press man and others displaying off man. This set up strongly suggests Cover 1.

The pre-snap Cover 1 train of thought for the quarterback needs to be that we are taking the top off the defense. Cover 1 plays man coverage underneath with a deep safety in the post. If the ball is rifled into the seam, the underneath corner will be able to undercut and intercept that throw. This ball needs to be aired out, away from the post safety, with enough room for the receiver to run underneath it.

The quarterback and receivers must be on the same page for this play to be successful. We cannot allow the post safety to cover both sluggos. The coaching note for the sluggo receivers is to break out of their route and drift away from the middle of the field. Their landmark is the imaginary line that evenly divides the area in between the hash and the numbers. This will take away the post safety's ability to play both routes. He is likely to commit to the boundary sluggo since that is the shorter – and typically easier – throw for the quarterback. Therefore, we should expect the field sluggo to be running free.

## POST-SNAP:

Utah's post-snap coverage is Cover 1 Hole. With the tight end and running back both running out routes, the middle linebacker becomes the hole player – a wasted defender versus this route concept. The sluggo receivers break off their slant routes and immediately drift to their landmarks. As indicated by our pre-snap read, the post safety commits to helping over the top of the boundary sluggo, leaving the Z receiver wide open for the 45-yard score.

What allowed this double-move route to be so successful was that the field corner was playing off-man technique. Off-man coverage defenders usually align in a 7x1 alignment – 7 yards off the ball and 1 yard inside the receiver. This technique is extremely susceptible to double moves because the space between the DB and the receiver entices the DB to jump the receiver's first move to avoid giving up a completion. That is exactly what occurs on this play. The Z breaks hard inside on his slant route, forcing the corner to try and cut it off. The receiver then sticks his foot in the ground a second time and gets vertical on his go route, making it impossible for the corner to recover. While this route works well against both press-man and off-man coverage, off-man puts the defense in the most vulnerable position.

## ADJUSTMENTS:

If our opponents rarely implement man-to-man defenses, this concept can still be successful in attacking single-high safety zone coverage such as Cover 3. To do this, we need to increase the depth of the slant routes to the point that they appear to be post routes. A quick, flatter-angled post route is commonly referred to as a bang post.

Zone defenders that are responsible for deep coverage will generally align 7-10 yards off the ball. In order to force them to bite on our in-breaking route, that route needs to be deep enough to threaten their zone. Many offenses install a 5-step bang post to beat Cover 3. The receiver's fifth step is planted between 7 and 10 yards, and by the time he catches the ball, he is perfectly placed between the corner, post safety, and underneath coverage linebacker. The only Cover 3 zone defender with a shot at breaking up this route is the deep 1/3 corner.

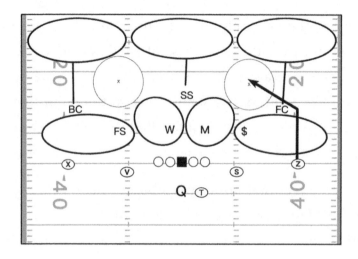

*Bang Post vs. Cover 3*

As with the sluggo set up, a few bang post completions in the soft spot of Cover 3 will be enough to force the corner's hand. He will bite on the next one, which will be our "bang post & go" for a long touchdown.

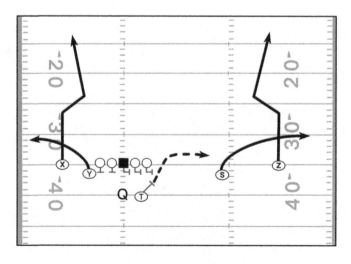

*Double Sluggo Adjustment, Bang Post & Go — Cover 3 Beater*

# 12

## RPO SLOT BUBBLE

### 2017 BIG 10 CHAMPIONSHIP

### THE OHIO STATE BUCKEYES VS. WISCONSIN BADGERS

**— CHAMPION —**

**THE OHIO STATE BUCKEYS**

# RPO SLOT BUBBLE

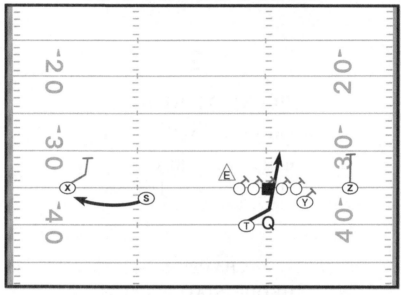

| POSITION | ALIGNMENT | ASSIGNMENT | COACHING NOTE |
|---|---|---|---|
| Q | GUN | RPO | READ BS EMLOS; CRASH = PULL & THROW, STAY = GIVE; CARRYOUT FAKE IF GIVE |
| T | SPLIT OG/OT; TOES TO HEELS | READ: PS-A, BS-A, BS-C | CARRYOUT FAKE IF QB PULL |
| X | FIELD TOP #s | BLOCK MDM | BE PATIENT COMING OFF THE BALL, WAIT FOR DEFENDERS TO DECLARE WHO WILL BE MDM |
| Z | BOUND. BOT. #s | BLOCK BC | RUN DB OFF IF PRESSED |
| S | FIELD HASH -1 | BUBBLE | MUST STAY BEHIND LOS; SECURE THE CATCH BEFORE GETTING EYES UP-FIELD |
| Y | I.S./O.S.; 1 YD BEHIND OT | INSIDE ZONE RT | BLOCK PS GAP DEFENDER OR DBL TEAM BS GAP DEFENDER |
| OL | BASE | IZ READ RT | BST LEAVE EMLOS |

FORMATION: GS DEUCE UP
PERSONNEL: 11
MOTION: N/A

## SCHEME:

This is an extremely popular concept in college football today, the RPO, or run pass option. Similar to the zone read runs that we broke down, RPOs execution depends on the decision made by the read defender. If that defender plays the run, the quarterback will pull the ball and throw the pass concept. If the read defender plays the pass, then the quarterback will carry out the handoff to the running back to execute the run concept.

The route concepts tagged to RPOs are generally easy throws with high completion rates such as slants, flats, and bubbles. The goal is to get the ball in our playmakers' hands as quickly as possible and allow them to do what they do best. The run concepts attached to RPOs tend to be basic zone schemes such as inside zone, outside zone, and split zone, but they can also be just as effective based on gap schemes like power and counter.

RPOs are most effective on base downs and 3$^{rd}$ & short situations, as both instances are reasonable for either the run or the pass. While they were not necessarily designed to result in explosive touchdowns, they can be lethal if the offense catches the defense in the wrong call.

Ohio State's RPO slot bubble concept is excellent to run if our opponent is weak on the perimeter. Perhaps their DBs are not physical enough to shed blocks and tackle. Maybe we have a speed advantage that we can exploit by getting to the outside. We may even just be in better shape than our opponent and we want to tire them out making them chase us the width of the field. Whatever our advantage may be, executing on the perimeter is a quick way to convert an easy completion into an explosive gain.

PRE-SNAP:

The Badgers decide to go with a double edge pressure, which they show pre-snap. A double edge pressure brings 2 defenders on a blitz from the same side of the ball. In this case, it's the nickel back and the strong safety. The pressure is given away because the free safety cheats over, aligning over #2 strong, and the strong safety is hard inside leverage of #2 strong with his eyes in the backfield. Anytime we see 2 defenders stacked on top of one another like this, we can assume that one of them is blitzing.

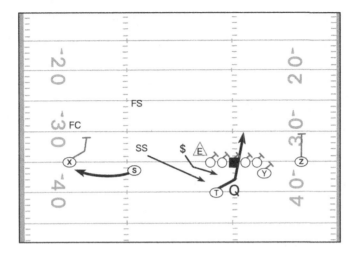

*Wisconsin Double Edge Pressure*

With both of the safeties tipping the blitz, we know that we're getting a Cover 0 look from the secondary – a man to man coverage with no deep safety help. The quarterback needs to be thinking 2 things: we should be throwing the pass concept versus the blitz, and the ball needs to be out quickly because Cover 0 equals a 6-man pressure.

POST-SNAP:

The job of the O-line on RPOs is to simply block the run concept. On this play, it is inside zone right. Even when the read dictates that the offense executes the pass concept, RPO throws are designed to be out quickly before any of the linemen can get a penalty for ineligible man downfield. The O-line's job is to run the D-line off the ball just as they would on any other run play. If we get called for an ineligible man downfield on an RPO, that's on the quarterback.

Understanding that the defensive EMLOS is the read defender, the backside tackle (backside of the run, not the throw) needs to leave him unblocked and work to the second level the same as he would on an inside zone read play. Seeing that Wisconsin's read defender blitzes, it's an easy pass read for the quarterback.

What springs this play for a 57-yard touchdown is the fact that Wisconsin's strong safety blitzes as well. This leaves the S receiver with 10 yards of space between himself and the safety guarding him.

The X's responsibility is to block MDM (most dangerous man) – whichever defender is the most immediate threat to tackling the ball carrier. Due to the abundant space in between the S and the free safety, the most dangerous man is the corner, and the X executes a textbook downfield block on him. Since the Badgers did in fact bring a Cover 0 blitz, the S now only has 1 man to beat until he's off to the races.

## ADJUSTMENTS:

There are numerous ways to manipulate the slot bubble concept to dial up the best results for your team. In accordance with our other read plays, we can easily eliminate the read for the quarterback by simply calling an automatic fake to the back followed by a throw to the bubble.

The slot bubble concept is also commonly run out of Trips, throwing the bubble to #3 strong. This adjustment provides us with an extra blocker on the perimeter, thus creating an extra running lane for the ball carrier.

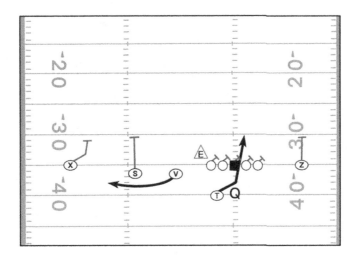

*RPO Slot Bubble out of 10 Personnel GS Trips*

However we choose to implement this concept, we must have sound blocking on the perimeter and speed at the slot position in order to turn this quick throw into an explosive, championship scoring play.

# HIGH RED ZONE
# SCORING RUNS

# 13

## QB DRAW

### 2018 SEC CHAMPIONSHIP

### ALABAMA CRIMSON TIDE VS. GEORGIA BULLDOGS

**— CHAMPION —**

**ALABAMA CRIMSON TIDE**

# QB DRAW

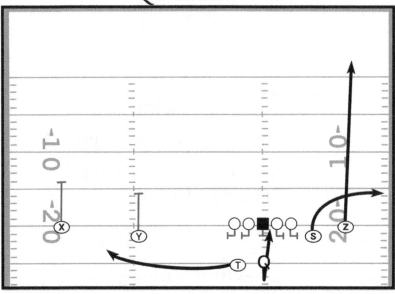

| POSITION | ALIGNMENT | ASSIGNMENT | COACHING NOTE |
|---|---|---|---|
| Q | GUN | DRAW | 1 STEP DROP; HIT EITHER OPEN A GAP; C WILL BLOCK MDM |
| T | BEHIND OT; EVEN WITH QB | SWING | MUST GET OUT QUICKLY TO WIDEN OUT LINEBACKERS |
| X | FIELD TOP #s | BLOCK FC | NEED THIS BLOCK TO SELL BUBBLE |
| Z | BOUND. BOT. #s | FADE | FADE TO FRONT PYLON TO PULL BC AWAY FROM MOF |
| S | DIV. EOL & Z | SPEED OUT | GET TO SIDELINE QUICKLY TO PULL FS AWAY FROM MOF |
| Y | DIV. EOL & X | BLOCK SAM/NICKEL | NEED THIS BLOCK TO SELL BUBBLE |
| OL | BASE | DRAW | G/T - SET IN LOCK PASS PRO, NO SLIDE, FORCE DEFENDERS INTO OUTSIDE GAPS; C - SET IN PASS PRO, BLOCK MDM FOR QB |

## FORMATION: GS DOUBLES
## PERSONNEL: 11
## MOTION: N/A

### SCHEME:

As offenses move into the red zone, quarterback runs become much more popular and much more effective. Due to the constricted space in the red zone, quarterbacks must make quicker decisions and more accurate throws. Many defenses respond to this by playing man coverage. However, man coverage takes the secondary's eyes off of the quarterback, leaving it solely up to the box defenders to stop the quarterback run.

By using the quarterback as a runner, we gain an extra blocker in the running back. This extra blocker gives us a numbers advantage against the box defenders. For example, if the defense needs to commit 6 defenders to stop the run against a traditional 10 personnel set, that provides them with 1 defender for each blocker, plus an extra defender to tackle the ball carrier. Now that our running back is a sixth blocker and the quarterback is the ball carrier, the defense must commit 7 defenders to stopping the run in order to maintain their numbers advantage.

If the defense must commit 7 box defenders to stop the quarterback run, they weaken their ability to play sound, red zone pass defense. No longer can they play man coverage with a post safety over the top because their post safety is now a box player. They must play Cover 0 if they are going to play man. In the case that they play Cover 0, we can exploit whichever DB/WR matchup is the most favorable to us.

Congruent with our other man-beating schemes, this QB draw scheme can be effective on any down. The main focus should be to hit it on a down and distance that screams man coverage for your opponent. We can set this play up by throwing the bubble screen to the running back a few times. That will generate the outside flow that we're looking for from the Mike linebacker.

Using the bubble screen to set this play up will also give us the best chance at beating zone coverage with it as well. The Mike does not have to immediately trigger on the bubble screen in zone coverage, but he will if we have hit it a few times for a 1st down.

PRE-SNAP:

Due to Alabama's ability to run the ball effectively relying solely on their 5 offensive linemen, Georgia sets up a 6-man box – a 4 down front and 2 linebackers. The defensive thought process here is, "as long as we have 1 more than they can block, we can stop the run." Alabama's answer to that is to remove one of Georgia's box players with a post-snap bubble by the running back, and then run with the quarterback.

Georgia's secondary is showing Cover 1 with a safety in the middle of the field and 1 defender matched up on each of Alabama's 4 vertical threats. This alerts the quarterback that 1 of the linebackers must be playing man on the running back and will follow him out of backfield – giving Bama the exact look that they hoped for.

## POST-SNAP:

Just as the Bulldogs' pre-snap look indicated, the Mike linebacker follows the running back's bubble to the field. The departure of this sixth box defender provides Alabama's offensive line with a 5-on-5 matchup against Georgia's remaining box defender. No longer does Georgia have 1 more than Alabama can block, and it's up to the secondary now to save the touchdown. However, the man coverage pulls the secondary's eyes away from the quarterback. The only defender with vision on the ball carrier is the deep post safety.

The difference between this Cover 1 scheme and many of the others that we've broken down throughout this book is the absence of the hole player. In the Cover 1 Hole scheme, one linebacker plays man on the back while the other sinks into the hole. But the Bulldogs elect to blitz their Will linebacker, forgoing the hole defender option in an effort to pressure the quarterback. This eliminates the second level of the defense, leaving nothing but green grass in between the quarterback and the distracted secondary.

In addition to manipulating the exodus of the box defenders, the receivers' routes are carefully designed to further widen the middle of the field. #1 and #2 weak run their DBs right out of the play. On the frontside, #1 and #2 strong pretend like they are blocking for the bubble to the back. This commits 3 players to defending that side of the play: the field corner, strong safety, and Mike linebacker. The only defender who is free to make the tackle on this play is the free safety; and he is 14 yards deep. 14 yards is plenty of space for an athletic quarterback to win that 1-on-1 matchup on his way into the end zone.

ADJUSTMENTS:

Many offenses will adjust this play by assigning the running back a TIF rope motion. This will generate pre-snap flow from the Mike linebacker and will create even more space for the quarterback to work with on the draw.

The rope motion will also indicate whether or not the defense is in man coverage. If the Mike linebacker follows the back out of the box, the defense is playing man. That is one less read that the quarterback has to make post-snap. Remember, the more post-snap reads we can convert into pre-snap reads, the simpler we make the game for our quarterback.

# 14

## INVERT INSIDE ZONE READ

### 2019 CFP CHAMPIONSHIP

### CLEMSON TIGERS VS. ALABAMA CRIMSON TIDE

**— CHAMPION —**

**CLEMSON TIGERS**

# INVERT INSIDE ZONE READ

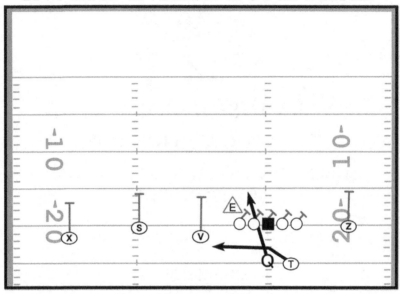

| POSITION | ALIGNMENT | ASSIGNMENT | COACHING NOTE |
|---|---|---|---|
| Q | GUN | READ PS EMLOS | CRASH = GIVE, STAY = KEEP; CARRYOUT FAKE IF GIVE |
| T | SPLIT OG/OT; EVEN WITH QB | PS D-GAP TO O.S. GAPS | HIT THE EDGE ASAP |
| X | FIELD TOP #s | BLOCK FC | RUN DB OFF IF PRESSED |
| Z | BOUND. BOT. #s | BLOCK BC | RUN DB OFF IF PRESSED |
| S | FIELD HASH; ON LOS | BLOCK SS | BLOCK OUTSIDE SHOULDER OF DEFENDER |
| V | DIV. EOL & S | BLOCK SAM/NICKEL | BLOCK OUTSIDE SHOULDER OF DEFENDER |
| OL | BASE | IZ READ RT; FIELD OT LEAVE EMLOS | ALTHOUGH WE'RE RUNNING LT, MUST BLOCK THIS LIKE IZ READ RT SO THAT THE FIELD EMLOS IS LEFT UNBLOCKED |

**FORMATION: GW TRIPS INVERT**
**PERSONNEL: 10**
**MOTION: N/A**

## SCHEME:

This zone read scheme is an excellent changeup from what most defenses are used to seeing. It is a simple inside zone read, but the quarterback's and running back's roles have been reversed. It is an exceptional way to confuse defenders and manufacture explosive plays even if the defense has the perfect call to potentially stop it.

As with our other zone read strategies, this call is best suited for base downs since it may be susceptible to a defense's 3$^{rd}$ down blitz tactics. Similar to other perimeter plays that we have analyzed, this concept will allow us to exploit any strength or speed advantages we have on the perimeter. Clemson clearly had the speed and strength perimeter advantage in this matchup as 2 Alabama DBs were blocked by Clemson receivers, and a third was outran by the running back on his way into the end zone.

Another great scenario in which we should run this play is if our quarterback is a more powerful runner than our running back, and our running back is a faster runner than our quarterback. If this is our situation, we may consider making this concept our base inside zone read scheme. SEC schools like Florida and Auburn won national championships a little over a decade ago basing their entire offensive philosophies on this concept. They had powerful runners at quarterback, and they terrorized opposing defenses week in and week out.

PRE-SNAP:

Alabama's defense is operating out of its dime package on this red zone play. Dime is a defensive personnel grouping that features 6 DBs on the field. It is a common counter to 10 personnel sets, since it gives the defense the best chance to match speed with speed in the passing game. In addition to the 6 DBs, Alabama is playing with 4 down D-linemen, and a Mike linebacker.

Starting out in a 2-high shell, the Tide's secondary begins a strong-side rotation just prior to the snap. This late rotation indicates pressure from the dime back as the strong safety stacks behind him and aligns with #3 strong. The pressure defender is the quarterback player, and the defensive EMLOS is the dive player. If this inside zone read was like all the rest, Alabama would have had this one wrapped up in the backfield. It is the invert aspect of this zone read that confuses the Alabama defense and leads to this 17-yard championship run.

There are 2 components of this zone read that invert the traditional concept. The first is the read defender identification. This scheme requires us to read the play side EMLOS, instead of the backside end man. Second, base zone reads feature the running back on the dive path and the quarterback on the bounce path, but this is the opposite. The running back takes the bounce path as if he were running outside zone. The quarterback, if his read dictates that he keep the ball, will run the dive path up the middle.

## POST-SNAP:

The reason we are still calling this play inside zone is because of the blocking scheme displayed by the O-line. The running back's path does not always dictate the run play, though it usually is an accurate tell. It is the O-line's blocking assignments that really indicate which run scheme the offense is executing.

Consistent with base inside zone read rules, the field tackle leaves his read defender 5 technique unblocked and works to the second level. The play side guard blocks his 3 technique. The center chips his backside shade and works to the second level. The backside guard blocks the shade aligned in his play side gap. And the backside tackle gap hinges his boundary 5 technique.

Despite the offensive line's best efforts, Alabama is still in good position to tackle this play for a loss because of the blitz that they sent. However, the inversion of the mesh point confuses the defenders in the backfield, and they allow the run to get outside of them. The read defender, who is supposed to be the dive player, does a good job staying home and playing the dive. But the quarterback defender, the blitzing dime player, follows the quarterback's dive path rather than peeling off onto the running back's bounce path. The Tide now have 2 dive defenders and no quarterback defender. This allows the running back to bounce outside and hit the perimeter with speed. A couple of solid perimeter blocks later by the X and S receivers and Clemson is up 6 in the national championship game.

## ADJUSTMENTS:

If reading the play side EMLOS is too difficult for our quarterback and running back to perform, we can change the read defender to a second level defender. It can be strenuous making the correct read when you're reading the defender that you are approaching; the read needs to happen so much faster because of how much quicker the space closes. By reading a second level defender, we buy more time for the quarterback to make an accurate read.

To make this adjustment, the play side tackle needs to block base inside zone rules. The new read defender will be the play side linebacker. If he flows outside of the play side tackle, that's a keep for the quarterback. If he stays inside the play side tackle, that's a give to the running back.

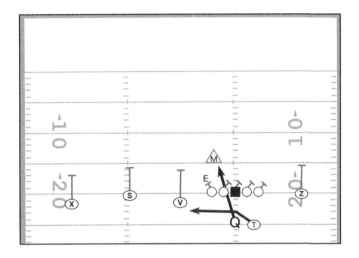

*Invert Inside Zone Read Adjustment — Read Second Level Defender*

# 15
## SPLIT ZONE
### 2019 ACC CHAMPIONSHIP
### CLEMSON TIGERS VS. VIRGINIA CAVALIERS

**— CHAMPION —**
**CLEMSON TIGERS**

# SPLIT ZONE

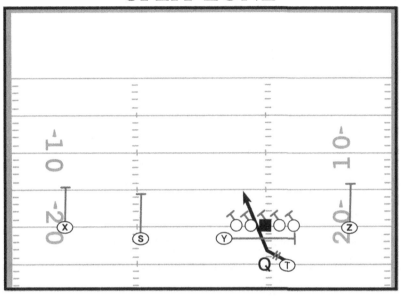

| POSITION | ALIGNMENT | ASSIGNMENT | COACHING NOTE |
|---|---|---|---|
| Q | GUN | GIVE TO T | CARRYOUT FAKE AFTER GIVE |
| T | SPLIT OG/OT; 1.5 YDS BEHIND QB | READ: PS-A, BS-A, BS-C | NO MORE THAN 1 CUT BEHIND LOS |
| X | FIELD TOP #s | BLOCK FC | RUN DB OFF IF PRESSED |
| Z | BOUND. TOP #s | BLOCK BC | RUN DB OFF IF PRESSED |
| S | FIELD HASH | BLOCK SAM/NICKEL | BLOCK INSIDE SHOULDER OF DEFENDER |
| Y | I.S./O.S.; 2 YDS BEHIND OT | BANG BLOCK DEFENSIVE EMLOS | STAY AS TIGHT TO LOS AS POSSIBLE, EMLOS MUST GO OVER THE BANG BLOCK |
| OL | BASE | SPLIT ZONE LT | BST LEAVE EMLOS; SAME BLOCKING SCHEME AS IZ LT W/ NO BS GAP HINGE |

**FORMATION: GW TREY UP**
**PERSONNEL:** 11
**MOTION:** N/A

## SCHEME:

Split zone is an excellent play to run when you have the same number of blockers as the defense has box defenders. This is due to the scheme's ability to create extra gaps post-snap. When the defensive box does not have a numbers advantage, it is absolutely vital that they fill every inside gap to avoid being tagged by explosive runs. The defense must have quick-thinking and even faster-reacting linebackers in order to properly fit up a run scheme that exchanges gaps post-snap. The odds of an inside gap being left unattended are rather high, and we must make them pay for such a critical mistake.

This is a great call on base downs and 3$^{rd}$ & short situations. On base downs, we are likely to see an equal number of box defenders to our blockers, providing us with the advantage we just discussed. But on 3$^{rd}$ & short, the defense is expecting run and will likely load to box to stop it. We can still use that to our advantage with this split zone scheme because the backside tackle will leave the EMLOS unblocked for the splitter. Leaving the edge defender unblocked for the splitter allows the backside tackle to block play side and may even provide us with an extra double team on the line of scrimmage. That extra line of scrimmage blocker and potential double team can be the difference between moving the chains on 3$^{rd}$ & short and punting.

PRE-SNAP:

Clemson begins this play with a favorable matchup as Virginia lines up in a 3-3-5 defense. With just 6 box defenders, the Cavaliers are outnumbered by Clemson's front. The Tigers' 5 offensive linemen and their tight end can block each of Virginia's D-linemen and linebackers. With no extra hat to account for the running back, he should be able to get to the secondary untouched. Seeing that Virginia's secondary is showing Cover 3 behind the 3-3 front, a clean running lane will put the back 1-on-1 with the post safety.

POST-SNAP:

Virginia's 3-man front versus this zone blocking scheme allows Clemson's O-line to generate quick knock back and work up to the second level. Since the back side EMLOS is playing a 4 technique over the tackle, base split zone rules indicate that he is the tackle's responsibility. If the defender were aligned in a 5 technique, then he would be in the tackle's back side gap and therefore, he would be the splitter's responsibility. Since that is not the case, the splitter must work up to the next outside defender, the Will linebacker.

With the splitter eliminating the Will, that leaves us with an interior 5-on-5 matchup. The back side guard does not have a play side gap defender since the nose guard is head up on the center. Therefore, he doubles the boundary 4 technique and works to the Mike linebacker in the second level. The center blocks the 0 technique nose guard. On the play side, our 2 O-linemen only have to worry about the Sam linebacker and the field 5 technique. Sticking with base rules, the play side tackle kicks out the field 5 technique and the play side guard works up to the Sam linebacker.

This is a great example of how split zone creates extra gaps post-snap to confuse the linebackers. Before the snap, the defense has to account for a field A-gap, B-gap, C-gap (between the tackle and tight end), and D-gap (outside the tight end). To the boundary, they only have to account for the A-gap, B-gap, and C-gap. Once the ball is snapped and the splitter crosses the formation, the D-gap to the field is lost, and the D-gap to the boundary is added. The addition of this gap causes the Will linebacker to fill the boundary D-gap, instead of his assigned C-gap. Upon noticing the absence of the C-gap defender, the Mike attempts to correct the Will's mistake and fills the C-gap himself. This over-correction leaves the backside A-gap unattended, resulting in the defense getting gashed for a 23-yard touchdown run.

## ADJUSTMENTS:

A common split zone variation is to run this scheme out of a 20 personnel 2-back set rather than the traditional 11 personnel set. The preferred backfield for this look is gun split – 2 backs on either side of the quarterback. The blocking scheme does not change at all when running this variation. The purpose is to confuse the defense with anonymity as to who will be the splitter and who will be the ball carrier. This ambiguity further delays the linebacker's recognition of any gaps that are either eliminated or created post-snap.

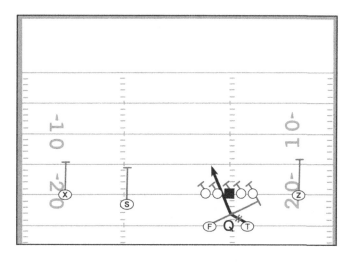

*Split Zone out of 20 Personnel G-Split Slot*

# HIGH RED ZONE
# SCORING PASSES

# 16

## RPO TE FLARE

### 2022 CFP CHAMPIONSHIP

### GEORGIA BULLDOGS VS. ALABAMA CRIMSON TIDE

**— CHAMPION —**
**GEORGIA BULLDOGS**

# RPO TE FLARE

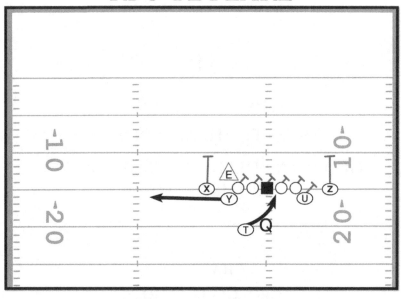

| POSITION | ALIGNMENT | ASSIGNMENT | COACHING NOTE |
|----------|-----------|------------|---------------|
| Q | GUN | RPO | READ DEFENSIVE EMLOS; CRASH = PULL & THROW, STAY = GIVE; CARRYOUT FAKE IF GIVE |
| T | SPLIT OG/OT; EVEN WITH QB | READ: PS-A, BS-A, BS-C | NO MORE THAN 1 CUT BEHIND LOS |
| X | MOF | BLOCK FC | RUN DB OFF IF PRESSED |
| Z | BOUND. TOP #s | BLOCK BC | RUN DB OFF IF PRESSED |
| Y | I.S./O.S.; TOES TO HEELS | FLARE SCREEN | WING STANCE; NOT A BUBBLE, LOOK FOR BALL OVER LEFT SHOULDER, MUST CATCH BEHIND LOS |
| U | I.S./O.S.; TOES TO HEELS | INSIDE ZONE RT | WING STANCE |
| OL | BASE | INSIDE ZONE READ RT | BST LEAVE EMLOS |

# FORMATION: GS ACE UP REDUCED
# PERSONNEL: 12
# MOTION: N/A

## SCHEME:

Down by 1 with less than 4 minutes to play in the national championship, Alabama desperately needs a stop. The Tide put nearly everybody on the line of scrimmage to defend against any run or quick throw. Georgia, on the other hand, has the perfect beater dialed up to extend their lead. This play is essentially a short yardage variation of Ohio State's RPO slot bubble concept that we analyzed a couple of chapters ago. In fact, Alabama is running the same defense that Wisconsin ran against the Buckeyes on that play.

As demonstrated by the National Champions, this is a great call on 3rd & short. As we analyze the defensive breakdown of this play, it may seem like it was only successful due to a coverage bust, but these busts happen regularly in big-time, short yardage situations such as this. Since the linebackers and safeties are so focused on their 3rd & short run-stopping responsibility, they often neglect their pass responsibility and lose containment of backs and tight ends leaking out of the backfield.

3rd & short is also a popular down and distance for defenses to send their double edge pressures because they are extremely difficult for O-linemen to block in the run game.

Defenses will almost always show their double edge pressures. Otherwise, they will not be able to get into the backfield quickly enough to disrupt the play.

Ideally, we will run the flare screen to the side that the blitz is coming from because that will provide the tight end with the most space to work with in his 1-on-1 matchup. Knowing this, a great way to assure that we get the right look is to teach our quarterback to audible and switch the play to the opposite side if our pre-snap read indicates a back side double edge pressure.

PRE-SNAP:

Since this is an RPO scheme, the quarterback must be keyed into his pre-snap read in order to simplify his post-snap read. The read defender is still the defensive EMLOS; this excludes secondary defenders that are in coverage. If the read defender chases the dive, we pull it and throw the flare screen to the tight end. If the read defender stays home, we give it to the back on the dive.

We must assume that on 3$^{rd}$ & 1 the read defender is chasing the dive. However, Alabama is showing a double edge field pressure, giving the quarterback even more reason to expect to throw this ball post-snap. Also running through the quarterback's mind must be the fact that double edge pressures send a dive player and a quarterback player, so the play action and throw to the tight end need to happen almost immediately.

Alabama makes it no secret that they are in Cover 0 as they bring their free safety into the box, on the field side of the Mike linebacker. The free safety, Mike, and Will are playing tango technique over Georgia's 3 backfield players – the 2 tight ends and the running back. Tango technique follows the same rules as banjo technique, the only difference is that tango indicates 3 defenders over 3 offenders as opposed to banjo's 2 over 2.

POST-SNAP:

Our pre-snap reads are confirmed by Alabama's post-snap movement. The nickel back and strong safety trigger on the blitz. Georgia's quarterback correctly reads the blitz and executes a quick play fake followed by an immediate throw to the tight end on the flare screen. The X receiver is able to get a good downfield block on the field corner since the corner is playing press-man. It is pivotal that the tight end runs the flare screen and catches the ball behind the line of scrimmage. Doing so allows the receiver to block the corner before the ball is caught. If the tight end catches the ball beyond the line of scrimmage while the receiver is blocking the corner, that will result in a 15-yard penalty.

The breakdown of the defense occurs when the free safety fails his tango assignment. His man is the tight end that flares out to his side, but he gets caught with his eyes in the backfield and is late to get out. Fortunately for Georgia, their tight end is fast enough to get up-field and outrun the pursuing safety into the end zone.

## ADJUSTMENTS:

As with many of our other zone reads and RPOs, if the read is too difficult for your quarterback, simply alter the play to an automatic play action pass. There is no sense in installing a complicated scheme to confuse the defense if it also causes confusion within the offense.

# 17

## PAP SPLIT ZONE BUFFALO

### 2020 PAC 12 CHAMPIONSHIP

### OREGON DUCKS VS. USC TROJANS

**— CHAMPION —**

**OREGON DUCKS**

# PAP SPLIT ZONE BUFFALO

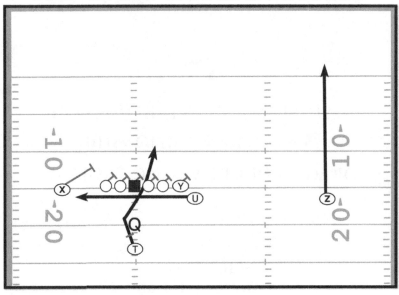

| POSITION | ALIGNMENT | ASSIGNMENT | COACHING NOTE |
|----------|-----------|------------|---------------|
| Q | GUN | PAP | MESH POINT LT EVEN THOUGH OL IS BLOCKING RT; SPRINT OUT LT WITH BUFFALO ROUTE |
| T | PISTOL; 2.5 YDS BEHIND QB | DIVE, CUTBACK, BOUNCE | OL BLOCKING SPLIT ZONE RT, PS A-GAP IS A-GAP TO THE RT |
| X | BOUND. TOP #s - 2 | CRACK BLOCK | CRACK THE MOST O.S. 2ND LEVEL DEFENDER (NOT INCLUDING THE CORNER) |
| Z | FIELD TOP #s | FADE | RUN DB OFF |
| Y | EOL | INSIDE ZONE RT | 3 PT. STANCE |
| U | I.S./O.S.; 1 YD BEHIND Y | BUFFALO | MUST CATCH BALL BEHIND LOS |
| OL | BASE | SPLIT ZONE RT; BST LEAVE EMLOS | BASE SPLIT ZONE RULES |

**FORMATION: PISTOL TREY WING**
**PERSONNEL: 12**
**MOTION: N/A**

## SCHEME:

Since this play is built off of a split zone look, we can run this play on any down and distance that we run our split zone scheme. The term buffalo is used to refer to a splitter's bluff block that turns into a flare screen.

As discussed in Michigan's bluff scheme, a bluff block is a fake bang block. Defenders who are bang block targets are generally taught to spill the block – which means to get underneath it. On the contrary, bang blockers are taught to force the defender over the top of the block. In order to create the most realistic bang block look, the bluff block tight end needs to stay tight to the line of scrimmage as if he were bang blocking and then avoid contact at the last second by allowing the defender to spill underneath him. Sound technique on the bluff block will allow the tight end a free release into the flare screen portion of his route.

## PRE-SNAP:

Oregon catches USC in the perfect storm with this buffalo scheme. To respond to the Ducks' 12 personnel set, USC brings their Sam linebacker down to press the Y off the line. They also bring their strong safety down, appearing to cover the U. However, the Trojans' safeties implement a 2-way coverage technique.

Similar to a banjo technique where 2 defenders play over 2 offenders, a 2-way consists of 2 defenders playing over 1 offender. Whichever side the offender releases to, the defender to that side will play him man to man, and the opposite side defender becomes a zone coverage defender.

In this scenario, the 2 safeties are playing a 2-way over the U. Whichever side the U releases to, the safety on that side will cover him; the other safety will roll into the post. USC does not concede this touchdown because of any mistakes they make pre-snap; rather, it is Oregon's post-snap execution that frees the tight end up for 6.

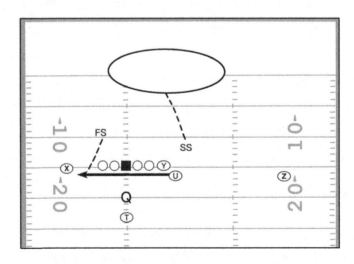

*USC 2-Way Coverage Technique*

## POST-SNAP:

As the U sprints across the formation post-snap, the strong safety (who had walked up on the line of scrimmage) loses ground and rolls into the post, causing the free safety to trigger down. Seeing the quarterback/running back mesh point in the backfield, the safety thinks that he has to play the run and spill the U's bang block. So, he quickly approaches the line of scrimmage and is blindsided by the crack block from the X receiver. This block seals the U's defender inside and allows the U to run free for a 16-yard touchdown after the catch. The post safety who had to roll from the opposite side of the field on the line of scrimmage is too far away to come over and prevent the score.

As with our last TE screen, this ball also needs to be caught behind the line of scrimmage to avoid a 15-yard penalty. The X receiver plays a pivotal role in the success of this play, because he has to draw 2 defenders away from the play. Not only does he have to crack the U's man, but his inside path needs to be convincing enough to cause the corner to follow him. The best way to accomplish this is to coach the receiver to perform the crack block the same way he would run a slant route. Oregon's X does a good job of this and by the time the tight end catches the ball, the corner is too far inside to make the tackle.

## ADJUSTMENTS:

The original play design suggests that the running back operates out of pistol alignment. Notice how the mesh point is to the left, but the O-line blocking scheme is split zone right. This is done to allow the quarterback an easy throw to the tight end after the play fake. However, it means that the running back's path needs to quickly shift from left to right as he aims for the play side A-gap.

In order to set this buffalo screen up, we need to give the defense the same look as we do when we run base split zone. If our playbook does not include a pistol package, then we should run this play out of a backfield set that we do use. This play can easily yield the same result by placing the back in a gun weak alignment.

# 18

## TE SLUGGO
### 2019 BIG 10 CHAMPIONSHIP
### THE OHIO STATE BUCKEYES VS. WISCONSIN BADGERS

**— CHAMPION —**

**THE OHIO STATE BUCKEYES**

# TE SLUGGO

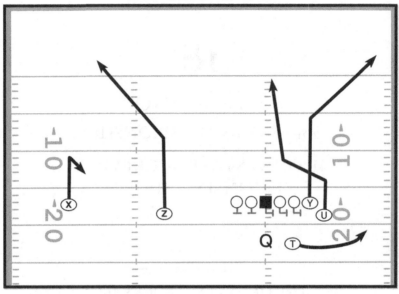

| POSITION | ALIGNMENT | ASSIGNMENT | COACHING NOTE |
|---|---|---|---|
| Q | GUN | DBP | MOFO READ - SLUGGO; MOFC READ - CORNERS |
| T | BEHIND OT; EVEN WITH QB | SWING | HOT ROUTE |
| X | FIELD TOP #s | 5-YD HITCH | WORK BACK INSIDE IF NOT IMMEDIATELY THROWN THE BALL |
| Z | FIELD HASH -2 | 10-YD CORNER | MOFO: FLATTEN TO SL; MOFC: AIM FOR BACK PYLON |
| Y | EOL | 10-YD CORNER | 3 PT. STANCE; O.S. RELEASE IF PRESSED |
| U | I.S./O.S.; 1 YD BEHIND Y | SLUGGO | BREAK ON SLANT ON 3RD STEP, BREAK ON GO ON 3RD STEP AFTER SLANT BREAK; DRIFT TO MOF |
| OL | BASE | 51 | PS = LT; 5-MAN PASS PRO; HALF SLIDE RT |

**FORMATION: GS DEUCE WING**
**PERSONNEL:** 12
**MOTION:** N/A

## SCHEME:

Hopefully it is clear by now that tight ends are major red zone assets. Because of their ability to block, and the defense's need to match personnel, tight ends often get matched up with linebackers and even D-line/linebacker hybrids. This is a solid matchup for the defense in the run game. But, anytime we recognize a matchup like that, we must exploit it in the passing game.

This tight-end-targeting concept is a multi-zone beater that will dissect any defensive scheme that leaves the middle of the field open (Cover 0, Cover 2, Cover 4). Against Cover 2, for example, the deep 1/2 safeties must follow the corner routes. Since the 3 hook/curl defenders all have underneath coverage responsibility, the top of their zones will not be deep enough to run with the TE sluggo, and that is who we hit for the touchdown.

Looking at this concept from a Cover 4 perspective – true quarters as opposed to match quarters – we may not be able to take the top off, but we will at least be able to move the chains. With the field corner dropping into his deep 1/4 zone, the hitch by #1 weak will be open all day. The field flat is neglected in Cover 4 because it is such a far throw for the quarterback. However, hitting one of your playmakers on a quick hitch in space may be just as deadly as airing it out into the end zone.

Due to the versatility of this route concept, it serves well as a base down and 3$^{rd}$ down call. Our best chances at getting the look we want from the defense are running this on base downs in the red zone, and on 3$^{rd}$ & short/medium in the open field. This is because when we go with 12 personnel, the defense is expecting run. They aren't necessarily expecting 2 tight ends to the same side to attack them vertically. If we can catch the defense thinking run in the red zone or on 3$^{rd}$ & short/medium in the open field, then we will get the mismatches we're looking for and hit this for an explosive touchdown.

PRE-SNAP:

Wisconsin shows an obvious pre-snap middle of the field open shell with both corners and both safeties indicating off-man coverage. In the box, the Badgers are in a 4-3 over front.

Our pre-snap read is screaming sluggo. When both the corners and the safeties are respectively aligned over the #1 and #2 receivers, that is a solid indicator that they are running some form of quarters coverage. Understanding that the safeties' responsibility in quarters is #2 vertical, we know that they both should follow the corner routes and further vacate the middle of the field.

POST-SNAP:

Despite no pre-snap indication of pressure, Wisconsin comes after the Buckeyes with a 5-man blitz, sending the Mike and Will and dropping the bandit into coverage. As the play unfolds, Wisconsin's secondary reveals that they are in fact playing match quarters. As is the case with fire zone matching, match quarters coverage consists of a final #3 player. Since the Mike and Will both blitz, the final #3 player is the Sam linebacker.

Every route in this concept is strategically designed to place secondary defenders in conflict and create open space for the offense to attack. The slant portion of the sluggo by #1 strong causes the corner to treat it as an under route and pass it off to the final #3 player while dropping to the deep part of his zone. As predicted, both corner routes by the #2 receivers pull the safeties away from the middle of the field. As the final #3 player pushes to his "underneath" threat, the tight end breaks up-field to complete his sluggo route and is wide open in the end zone.

ADJUSTMENTS:

As previously mentioned, having 2 tight ends who can threaten vertically is a luxury that not all teams have. That will not stop us from successfully implementing this concept. Many teams have had success placing a second running back or a third receiver at the U position. This provides more speed with which we can attack the middle of the field with that sluggo route.

However, if we are going to make this personnel switch, we cannot let it affect our ability to run the ball out of this formation. It is our run threat that provides us with a mismatch in the passing game. If our run threat is eliminated, then our pass threat is vanquished as well. Whichever skill position replaced the U must be able to block effectively.

# 19
## SLANT/BUBBLE
### 2021 ACC CHAMPIONSHIP
### PITTSBURGH PANTHERS VS. WAKE FOREST DEMON DEACONS

**— CHAMPION —**

**PITTSBURGH PANTHERS**

# SLANT/BUBBLE

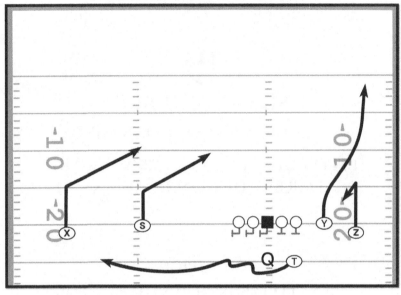

| POSITION | ALIGNMENT | ASSIGNMENT | COACHING NOTE |
|---|---|---|---|
| Q | GUN | DBP | MAN READ - BUBBLE; ZONE READ - CURL/FLAT ZONE DEFENDER |
| T | BEHIND OT; 1 YD BEHIND QB | ROPE MOTION; SWING | WORK BACK TO 5 YDS BEHIND LOS, SHOULD CATCH 3-4 YARDS BEHIND LOS |
| X | FIELD TOP #s | 5-STEP SLANT | MUST THREATEN VERTICALLY IN 1ST 5 STEPS TO FORCE DB'S TO RETREAT AS MUCH AS POSSIBLE |
| Z | BOUND. BOT. #s | 5-YD HITCH | OFF LOS |
| S | FIELD HASH | 5-STEP SLANT | MUST THREATEN VERTICALLY IN 1ST 5 STEPS TO FORCE DBs TO RETREAT AS MUCH AS POSSIBLE |
| Y | BOUND. TOP #s -1; ON LOS | FADE | FADE TO DIV. #s & SL |
| OL | BASE | 50 | PS = RT; 5-MAN PASS PRO; HALF SLIDE LT |

**FORMATION: GW DOUBLES INVERT**
**PERSONNEL:** 11
**MOTION: TIF ROPE**

## SCHEME:

Due to the regularity of man defense on 3<sup>rd</sup> down and in the red zone, this is a great call on 3<sup>rd</sup> & medium as well as high red zone base downs. We do not need to worry about a 3<sup>rd</sup> down blitz affecting the success of this play since the goal is to get the ball out to the back as quickly as possible.

With that being said, we still need to note that the back exiting the backfield leaves us with just a 5-man protection. So, if for some reason the defense does have the back covered, we cannot afford to hold onto the ball or else we will be sacked in the even of a blitz. Sacks in the high red zone are devastating for offenses as they can potentially take us out of field goal range. We need to be fast and accurate with our decisions at the quarterback position to make this play a success.

## PRE-SNAP:

Wake Forest shows a pre-snap 4-2-5 Cover 1 Hole look. Each DB playing with man eyes over their receiver should tell our quarterback we are throwing it to the back. The route concept on this play aims at exploiting the linebacker on running back mismatch. Against man coverage, the 2 field DBs should follow the slant routes inside, providing the back with plenty of space to work with on the outside. The key to realizing this concept is the pre-snap rope motion. This motion gets the back moving full speed at the snap of the ball, providing him with both a leverage and speed advantage on his man defender.

POST-SNAP:

With the back swinging out to the field, banjo rules indicate that the Mike now has the back man-to-man and the Will is now the hole player. At the snap of the ball, the Mike linebacker gives the nickel (the DB guarding 2 strong) a push call. Push calls indicate an exchange from the #2 and #3 receivers. The defender receiving the push call must come off his #2 receiver and push to the #3 receiver heading his direction. The defender giving the push call abandon's his out-breaking path on the #3 receiver and instead picks up the #2 receiver breaking inside. A push call is the defense's only chance at stopping this play out of man coverage. Fortunately for Pitt, the push call does not get communicated effectively, and both the nickel and the mike pick up the slant by #2 strong. This leaves absolutely nobody in the vicinity of the back, and he is able to walk in for the 22-yard score.

Even if the defense were able to perform the push call correctly, this play is designed to still have options. By passing the slant by #2 strong off to the Mike linebacker and playing the swing route, the nickel increases the space that the offense has to complete the slant to #1 strong. The X just has to win on the inside, and we will have an easy 1$^{st}$ down completion.

The quarterback's read progression is bubble, outside slant, inside slant, slot fade, boundary hitch. As coaches, we must convey to our players the importance of every route in the quarterback's read progression. These route concepts are expertly crafted in a way that when one door closes, another one opens. They will yield results as long as all 11 do their job.

## ADJUSTMENTS:

While this play is an obvious man beater, we can adjust the strong-side route concept to modify this play into a 1-high zone (Cover 3) beater as well. The purpose of doing so is to assure a completion in space to the back.

To do this, we need to still be able to occupy the 2 field DBs. The field corner's Cover 3 responsibility is deep 1/3, and nickel's is curl/flat. When faced with a high/low route concept, defenders are taught to take away the high route first, and then come down and tackle the low route if the ball is thrown there. We can easily capitalize on that teaching with this scheme. A simple go route by the X and a 10-yard curl by the S will force both of these defenders to hold the high end of their zones before coming down on the swing route. This will still provide the back with plenty of space to make an uncontested catch and get up-field.

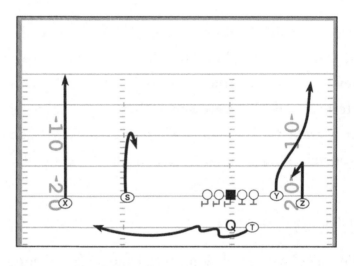

*Slant/Bubble Adjustment — Cover 3 Beater*

# 20

## PAP POST/WHEEL

### 2018 BIG 10 CHAMPIONSHIP

### THE OHIO STATE BUCKEYES VS. NORTHWESTERN WILDCATS

**— CHAMPION —**

**THE OHIO STATE BUCKEYES**

# PAP POST/WHEEL

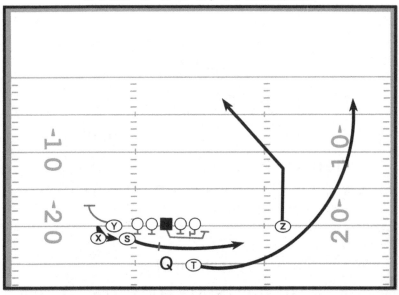

| POSITION | ALIGNMENT | ASSIGNMENT | COACHING NOTE |
|---|---|---|---|
| Q | GUN | PAP | FAKE JET SWEEP TO S; 1ST READ - POST, 2ND READ - WHEEL |
| T | SPLIT OG/OT; HEELS TO TOES | WHEEL | WORK TO DIV. #s & SL ON WHEEL ROUTE |
| X | 1 YD O.S. & BEHIND Y | NOW ROUTE | 1 VERTICAL STEP, COME BACK TO LOS AND SIT; NOT A TUNNEL SCREEN |
| Z | FIELD HASH +1 | 8-YD POST | PULL POST SAFETY AND FC |
| S | 1 YD I.S. & BEHIND Y | FAKE JET SWEEP | AFTER FAKING SWEEP, BUBBLE TO FIELD TO GIVE QB CHECK DOWN ROUTE |
| Y | EOL +2 | BLOCK MDM | ARC RELEASE; BLOCK 1-2 YDS MAX IN FRONT OF LOS |
| OL | BASE | JET SWEEP PASS PRO | BSG, BST, & PSG LOCK; PST SLIDE LT & PROTECT I.S. GAP; C PULL & PROTECT PS C-GAP |

## FORMATION: GW TRIPS BUNCH REDUCED
## PERSONNEL: 11
## MOTION: N/A

### SCHEME:

This is primarily a base down call due to the various eye candy concepts that are involved. The post-snap, fake jet sweep forces us to call this play on a down that is also a realistic running down for us. Same with the now screen to the X receiver. Now screens and jet sweeps are not typical 3$^{rd}$ down passing situation calls, but they are extremely common on base downs.

While the now screen and fake jet are not necessarily essential to the overall scheme of this specific play, they do play an important role in setting this play up. Ohio State has multiple variations of this play. One in which they hand the ball off to the jet, and another one where they fake the jet and throw the now screen. These additional plays are must-haves if you wish to successfully install the explosive post/wheel variation.

### PRE-SNAP:

Northwestern shows a 2-high shell out of a 4-3 personnel package. The corners are indicating zone coverage as they are both angled towards the middle of the field with their eyes on the quarterback. If the 2-high coverage remains true post-snap, then we will be getting either Cover 4 or Cover 2 from the defense. Cover 4 does not look promising, seeing that they have 2 deep defenders to the field to cover both of our deep routes. Cover 2, on the other hand, could lead to something big.

The post/wheel concept is a solid Cover 2 beater because it send 2 receivers into the deep ½ player's zone. With the running back releasing vertically from the backfield, the safety does not see him as an immediate threat, so he will squeeze to the post. Base zone coverage rules state that you should always take the second man to run through your zone. For the Cover 2 corner, the running back is that second man, so he should follow the wheel route. However, it's extremely common for flat defenders to leave wheel routes unattended, thinking that they are just passing them off to the deep coverage defender behind them. Even if the corner does run with the wheel, he will be trailing it rather than playing over the top since he is an underneath defender. With the safety occupied by the post, the underneath corner has no over-the-top help and we can put this ball in the back of the end zone for the back to run under.

The reduced set is one of the keys to success on this play. If Ohio State was in a regularly spread formation, the running back would not be able to get outside of the defense quickly enough, and another DB may be able to come over and make the play. By condensing the formation and then running an in-breaking route with the Z, we give our back ample opportunity to get outside and work with as much space as possible.

POST-SNAP:

The Wildcats end up running a completely different coverage scheme than what our pre-snap read indicated. Fortunately, the coverage that they do run – Cover 1 – is even more vulnerable to this post/wheel concept. Since Northwestern begins in a 2-high shell, they need a post-snap safety rotation in order to get to Cover 1. They run a weak side safety rotation, meaning that the safety to the weak side of the formation is the one that comes down and plays underneath, while the strong side safety rotates back into the post.

The weak side rotation plays into the Buckeyes' favor because, as Northwestern's safety is coming downhill to cover the back man to man, Ohio State's back is releasing vertically at full speed. Needing to change directions in man coverage that quickly is difficult for any DB. The field corner cannot help over the top because he is trailing the post man to man. And the middle of the field safety cannot come over and help on top of the wheel because he must protect the inside post first. This allows Ohio State's quarterback to throw the ball into the end zone with some air under it, resulting in a routine touchdown catch for the back.

## ADJUSTMENTS:

In order to best disguise the actual jet sweep with this play action variation, the blocking schemes must appear as parallel as possible. The pulling center is a common gap blocking scheme for sweeps. That is why this play features a pulling center in pass protection.

In the event that we hand the ball off on the jet sweep, the pulling center is the lead blocker. He should either look to kick out the play side tackle's play side gap defender or wrap to the second level and seal any linebackers scraping over the top. The second lead blocker is the running back. Pulling the center in protection, and releasing the back on a wheel route gives the appearance of Ohio State's 2-lead blocker jet sweep scheme.

However, many teams will block jet sweep the same way they block outside zone. No matter which jet sweep blocking scheme is best for our team, we must use the same scheme for the protection of this post/wheel concept in order to keep the defense honest.

# 21

## RB ANGLE
### 2020 SEC CHAMPIONSHIP
### ALABAMA CRIMSON TIDE VS. FLORIDA GATORS

**— CHAMPION —**
**ALABAMA CRIMSON TIDE**

# RB ANGLE

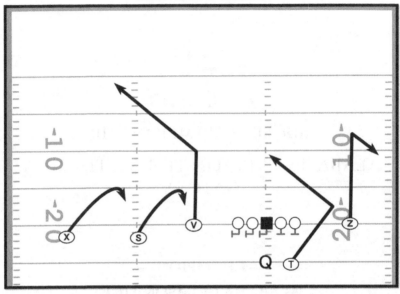

| POSITION | ALIGNMENT | ASSIGNMENT | COACHING NOTE |
|---|---|---|---|
| Q | GUN | DBP | READ LT SIDE 1ST; MAN READ - CORNER; ZONE READ - SNAGS; ANGLE IS 3RD READ |
| T | SPLIT OG/OT; EVEN WITH QB | ANGLE | CUT UNDERNEATH DEFENDER WHEN BREAKING BACK INSIDE; NOT A REVERSE PIVOT TO QB |
| X | FIELD TOP #s | 5-YD SNAG | FIND OPEN SPOT IN ZONE |
| Z | BOUND. BOT. #s | 12-YD COMEBACK | BREAK AT 12 YDS, HIT THE SIDELINE AT 9 |
| S | FIELD HASH | 5-YD SNAG | FIND OPEN SPOT IN ZONE |
| V | DIV. HASH & EOL | 10-YD CORNER | ON LOS; MOFO: FLATTEN TO SL; MOFC: SKINNY TO BACK PYLON |
| OL | BASE | 50 | PS = RT; 5-MAN PASS PRO; HALF SLIDE LT |

**FORMATION: GW TREY FLEX**
**PERSONNEL: 10**
**MOTION: N/A**

## SCHEME:

Angle routes are extremely effective against man coverage, making them great calls on 3$^{rd}$ down and in the red zone. They are also effective against zone coverages as the out-breaking portion of the route spans far enough outside for the hook coverage defender to pass it off to the curl/flat defender. As the back breaks back inside, he will catch ball right in between the hook and curl passing zones.

Alabama provides us with an excellent 2-minute concept with this play. If we want to be a championship offense, we must be able to put points on the board in 2-minute situations. Our game plan for each week should consist of designated plays that we will call during the 2-minute drill, should we find ourselves in that situation. Alabama's RB angle concept needs to be on that menu.

At the high school and college levels, a first down stops the clock long enough for the chains to reset. In a 2-minute scenario, coverage defenders will generally play a few yards deeper than normal to avoid getting beat deep. Their loose coverage will provide us with enough space to complete this angle route right around the first down marker, allowing the back an opportunity to make a play in space, moving the chains and stopping the clock — or in this case, putting 6 points on the board.

PRE-SNAP:

On the plus 17-yard line, 13 seconds remaining in the half and only 1 timeout, Alabama is in a must-pass situation if they wish to come away with a touchdown before entering the locker room. Florida's strategy is to play deep coverage, accompanied by a blitz. The blitz will force Alabama to get rid of the ball quickly, allowing the deep Gator defenders to rally down and make the tackle in bounds.

They show a 2-high shell with both corners at least 10 yards off the ball, indicating Cover 4. Up-front, the Gators bring 6 defenders up on the line of scrimmage. This is a good indicator that the blitz is coming, but it is not a sure tell. Defenses will often show a 6-man pressure but end up only bringing 3. They may even blitz the linebackers and drop a defensive lineman or 2 into zone coverage, hoping to force the quarterback into a costly mistake. It is important for the quarterback to keep his eyes on his blitz read defenders so that he knows which ones are actually coming and which ones are dropping into coverage. This will indicate to him the amount of time he should expect to have to throw.

POST-SNAP:

The Gators end up sending 5 on the blitz and dropping 1 of their walked-up linebackers into coverage. This linebacker's responsibility is to relate to the back. He does not need to deny the back the ball; he just needs to be able to prevent the back from creasing the defense with yards after the catch. The remaining Florida defenders drop into their true Cover 4 zones.

The 5-man rush from the Gators does a good job scheming up 2 untouched pass-rushers and they force a quick throw from the quarterback as intended. The break down occurs in the 1-on-1 linebacker/running back matchup. Although the linebacker simply needs to relate to the back, he bites hard on the out-breaking portion of the angle route and is unable to contain the back once he breaks back inside. With the deep 1/4 safeties playing a couple yards deep into the end zone, they are unable to make contact with the back until the 2-yard line – not enough space to keep this playmaker out of the end zone.

## ADJUSTMENTS:

The purpose of this play is to capitalize on the 1-on-1 matchup between the running back and the linebacker. If we are playing against a linebacker that refuses to give up his inside leverage, we can convert this angle route into a simple flat route. This would also force us to switch the Z's route as well. The comeback route restricts the space that the back has to work with post-catch. By sending the Z on a fade route, that will clear out the boundary enough to comfortably hit the back in the flat.

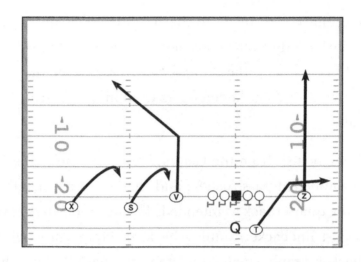

*RB Angle Adjustment — Inside Leverage Beater*

# 22

## STICK/SMASH
### 2020 CFP CHAMPIONSHIP
### LSU TIGERS VS. CLEMSON TIGERS

**— CHAMPION —**
**LSU TIGERS**

# STICK/SMASH

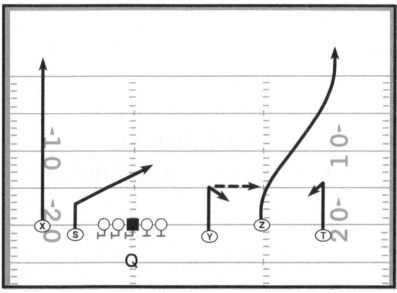

| POSITION | ALIGNMENT | ASSIGNMENT | COACHING NOTE |
|---|---|---|---|
| Q | GUN | QUICK GAME | 1ST READ - SLOT FADE; 2ND READ - STICK; 3RD READ - SLANT |
| T | FIELD TOP #s | 5-YD HITCH | OFF LOS |
| X | BOUND. BOT. #s | FADE | HOLD BOTTOM #s UNTIL BALL TAKES YOU OFF |
| Z | FIELD HASH | FADE | ON LOS; FADE TO FRONT PYLON |
| S | DIV. EOL & X | 3-STEP SLANT | MUST WIN ON THE INSIDE |
| Y | DIV. EOL & HASH | 5-YD STICK | MAN COVERAGE = CONTINUE TO SIDELINE ZONE COVERAGE = SIT IN OPEN ZONE |
| OL | BASE | 50 | PS = RT; 5-MAN PASS PRO; HALF SLIDE LT |

# FORMATION: EMPTY TRIPS INVERT
# PERSONNEL: 11
# MOTION: N/A

## SCHEME:

This passing scheme contains multiple route concepts that are must-haves in any offense's quick game arsenal. This 2-for-1 strategy provides the offense with multiple answers to multiple defensive schemes. The two concepts are stick and smash.

The stick route is run by the tight end. It is a 5-yard hitch that turns to the outside instead of the inside. The dotted lines indicate an option route for the tight end, allowing him to attack the weakness of whichever coverage the defense is in. If the defense is playing man, then the tight end will turn the hitch into an out route and attempt to outrun his man coverage defender to the sideline. If the tight end gets a zone coverage read, then he will run the hitch as indicated and sit in the open zone. The stick concept is commonly run out of 3x1 formations with #3 strong running the stick route. But the route does not always have to be run by a tight end. It should be executed by whichever skill player provides the best matchup.

The smash concept is another common scheme that succeeds against man and zone coverages. It consists of a short route by #1 (usually a 5-yard hitch), and a vertical, out-breaking route by #2. The most common smash out-breaking route is a corner route, although the slot fade is a close second. Both routes aim to attack the same zone. The design was originally installed to attack the Cover 2 soft spot just over the flat corner and underneath the deep ½ safety. While still a solid Cover 2 beater, this concept has become extremely popular to attack the weakness of Cover 1 as well. A fade is much more difficult to cover from the slot than out wide because the offense has much more space to complete the pass, as seen with LSU on this play.

Smash can even be effective against Cover 3 and Cover 4. Our deep route will most likely be covered, but both of those coverages require the corner to squeeze to the vertical, freeing up the hitch. It's not an explosive play design against these coverages, but it gets the job done and moves the chains.

Since LSU has built into this play multiple concepts to beat multiple coverages, the pre-snap read becomes the key to success. As long as our quarterback is sound with his pre-snap read, we will be just fine. Even if the defense runs something post-snap that is different than what our pre-snap read indicated, there is no need to panic because we will have an open receiver on this play.

The challenge with this play is that the quarterback's decision needs to be made quickly since we are operating out of an empty set. Defenses love to blitz empty sets because they know they are only getting a 5-man protection. Still, both the stick and smash concepts are quick game schemes with the potential to beat any blitz.

## PRE-SNAP:

Clemson's pre-snap look heavily indicates Cover 1. Each LSU receiver is accounted for by a Clemson DB, backed up by a single-high post safety. Additionally, Clemson shows blitz by walking both of their linebackers up to the line of scrimmage and inserting them on either side of the 0 technique in this 3-down front. The walked-up linebackers should alert the quarterback that there may not be a hole player in this defense.

The quarterback's pre-snap read progression should be slot fade, stick, weak side slant. Against man coverage, we always want our deep ball to be the first read. We will know within the first second to second and a half of the play if the deep shot is there or not. If it is, we have to capitalize on it. The stick concept is the second read because it is the closest man-beating route to the slot fade, making it easy for the quarterback to shift his eyes that direction. The weak side slant is the third read because it is a man beater that passes right through the low hole, which appears to be vacated by the blitzing linebackers, but we will not be certain of that until after the snap.

## POST-SNAP:

Clemson ends up blitzing both linebackers, but dropping the nose guard into coverage to play the low hole. The 2 short routes by #1 and #3 strong assure that the post player is the only threat to taking away our shot to #2 strong on the slot fade. In order to eliminate the post safety threat, the S must angle his fade route about 4 yards inside of the front pylon. Any further inside and we may be throwing a pick.

The short pylon path also offers the quarterback the option to either lead the receiver to the back of the end zone or throw him a back shoulder fade on the sideline. The ball placement depends on the positioning of the man coverage defender. If the DB is underneath and trailing the receiver, it's best to lead the receiver and allow him to run underneath it. If the DB is even or over the top of the receiver, then we want to aim for the receiver's back shoulder. Clemson's DB is even with the receiver when LSU's quarterback lets it fly. The ball travels to the receiver's back shoulder, just inside the short pylon, and LSU puts the dagger in the national championship game.

## ADJUSTMENTS:

LSU uses 11 personnel to operate this play out of an empty set, placing their back at #1 strong. This was beneficial to LSU because their back was a major threat in the passing game all year long. If our running back is not involved in our base passing attack, it does us no good to split him out wide; he will not draw the attention that position requires. We can easily adjust the personnel to better suit our team's strengths. The defense is already keyed into the pass out of an empty set, so we need to assure that our best 5 passing threats are in the game.

# 23
## MESH
### 2019 BIG 10 CHAMPIONSHIP
### THE OHIO STATE BUCKEYES VS. WISCONSIN BADGERS

**— CHAMPION —**
**THE OHIO STATE BUCKEYES**

# MESH

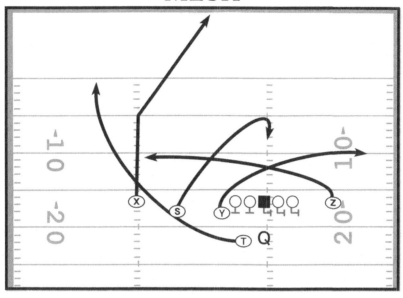

| POSITION | ALIGNMENT | ASSIGNMENT | COACHING NOTE |
|----------|-----------|------------|---------------|
| Q | GUN | DBP | 1ST READ - OTB; 2ND READ - MESH; 3RD READ - POST/WHEEL |
| T | SPLIT OG/OT; EVEN WITH QB | WHEEL | DIV. HASH & #s ON WHEEL ROUTE |
| X | FIELD HASH | 10-YD POST | BIG POST, TAKE THE TOP OFF |
| Z | BOUND. BOT. #s | MESH | UNDERNEATH ON MESH; ZONE = MOTOR DOWN IN MOF & FIND OPEN ZONE, MAN = KEEP RUNNING |
| S | DIV. X & Y | 10-YD OTB (OVER THE BALL) | SIT DOWN IN THE OPEN ZONE |
| Y | 1 YD O.S. & BEHIND OT | MESH | OVER THE TOP ON MESH; ZONE = MOTOR DOWN IN FLAT & FIND OPEN ZONE, MAN = KEEP RUNNING |
| OL | BASE | 51 | PS = LT; 5-MAN PASS PRO; HALF SLIDE RT |

**FORMATION: GS TREY UP**
**PERSONNEL: 11**
**MOTION: N/A**

SCHEME:

Mesh is a classic concept with a wide variety of targets. Many offenses prefer to run their mesh concept on 3$^{rd}$ down, but it works just as well on base downs. While many believe that mesh is a man-beating concept, it was originally conceived by the air raid pioneers to beat zone coverage. It was designed to work exactly how the Buckeyes executed it in this BIG 10 Championship game. The mesh routes are supposed to lure the underneath coverage defenders out of their middle zones so that we can have a clear lane to the OTB (over the ball) route. If the middle-zone defenders stay home and sink under the OTB, then we can hit 1 of the mesh routes before it reaches the next coverage zone.

Although this concept was designed to manipulate zone coverage, we can expect to have success with is versus man coverage as well. Any 2 crossing routes are reliable man-beaters. Similar to our deep over routes, it is extremely difficult for any man defender to run with a receiver all the way across the field.

If our mesh concept does not free up an open man, we should have a favorable matchup with our running back on the wheel route. In fact, the post/wheel concept is also an additional zone beater against Cover 3. Post/wheel concepts have been terrorizing Cover 3 corners for years. For a deep 1/3 corner, squeezing to that post is so enticing that they completely miss the wheel route sneaking behind them.

With various coverage beating concepts built into this one scheme, mesh is a must-have in any championship offense.

## PRE-SNAP:

Wisconsin shows a single-high safety look pre-snap, with the boundary corner pressed and the field corner 10 yards deep, showing zone. This appears to be the same Cover 3 variation that Ohio State ran against Alabama's slot deep over, with the corner to the back side of the 3x1 formation playing man coverage.

However, if we see the 3x1 backside corner pressed against our receiver, we cannot automatically assume that he will be playing man. Defenses will often disguise their Cover 3 look with what is called press-bail technique. This means that the corner shows press pre-snap, but quickly bails into a true Cover 3 deep 1/3 zone post-snap. The point of this technique is to take away any quick throws to the outside, without sacrificing deep ball security. It is important to get a pre-snap read on both corners when the defense is in a single-high set. If they are showing opposing looks, then we need to be extra keyed into our post-snap read.

As far as our box pre-snap read is concerned, the Badgers show a 4-down front with 2 stand-up defensive ends – a heavy indication of pass rush so we should expect them to game our offensive line. The Will linebacker walks up to the line just before the snap, inserting himself between the 2 defensive tackles. When a linebacker or safety waits until just before the snap to walk up to the line, we have to assume that they are coming. If they don't, they run a huge risk of being out of position when dropping back into coverage.

POST-SNAP:

At the snap of the ball, the boundary corner bails into his deep 1/3 zone, confirming press-bail technique and true Cover 3. The walked-up Will linebacker does in fact blitz, but the boundary defensive end drops into coverage, solidifying a 4-man rush. The 2 mesh routes do a good job drawing the middle, underneath defenders out of their zones, which leads to an easy pitch and catch to the OTB.

After securing the catch and turning up-field, the S just has to make the post safety miss before diving into the end zone and giving his team a late third quarter lead in the conference championship.

ADJUSTMENTS:

There are a million ways to run mesh – 3x1, 2x2, 10 personnel, 11 personnel, etc. Ohio State's mesh concept embodies the original and most common design. Offensive coordinators who build their passing scheme off of mesh will find a way to run the same concept out of different formations and personnel groupings. We have the freedom to play around with the various route combinations involved in mesh in order to find the best fit for our team.

# 24
## CROSS COUNTRY
2020 SEC CHAMPIONSHIP

ALABAMA CRIMSON TIDE VS. FLORIDA
GATORS

**— CHAMPION —**
**ALABAMA CRIMSON TIDE**

# CROSS COUNTRY

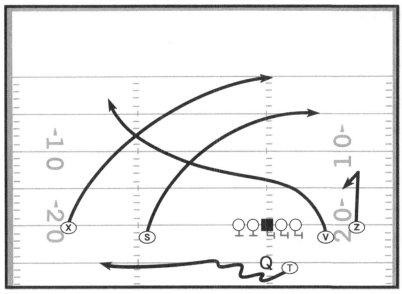

| POSITION | ALIGNMENT | ASSIGNMENT | COACHING NOTE |
|---|---|---|---|
| Q | GUN | DBP | MOFO READ - DEEP OVER; MOFC READ - CURL/FLAT DEFENDER (IF ZONE) |
| T | SPLIT OG/OT; TOES TO HEELS | ROPE MOTION; SWING | MAINTAIN 5 YDS BEHIND LOS |
| X | FIELD TOP #s | DEEP OVER | FLATTEN OUT AT 20 YDS; WORK MOF IF QB BEGINS TO SCRAMBLE |
| Z | BOUND. BOT. #s | 7-YD HITCH | WORK UP THE SIDELINE IF QB BEGINS TO SCRAMBLE |
| S | FIELD HASH -1 | DEEP OVER | FLATTEN OUT AT 15 YDS; WORK BACK TO QB IF HE BEGINS TO SCRAMBLE |
| V | DIV. EOL & Z | BENDER | UNDER SAM/NICKEL & OVER MIKE; AIM FOR 18-20 YARDS; KEEP CLIMBING VERTICALLY |
| OL | BASE | 51 | PS = LT; 5-MAN PASS PRO; HALF SLIDE RT |

**FORMATION: GW DOUBLES**
**PERSONNEL: 10**
**MOTION: TIF ROPE**

## SCHEME:

This Alabama cross-country concept is designed to attack the same field zone as their slot deep over concept that we previously analyzed. The difference here is that this concept is designed to beat a 2-high shell, whereas the slot deep over targets a 1-high shell.

This is a great high red zone concept because quarters coverage is common in this area. The goal from the defensive perspective is that by playing Cover 4, they shrink the already-constricted space in the red zone and force the quarterback to throw the ball into tighter windows. Such was not the case on this occasion. This scheme is an excellent way to expand the shrinking throwing windows in the red zone.

While the purpose of this play is to beat 2-high safety zone coverages, it can be successful against man as long as our V receiver is fast enough to beat his man across the field. Man coverage will result in the same zone opening up as the man defenders on #1 and #2 strong will chase them across the field.

The coverage-beating versatility of this scheme makes this play a serviceable call on either base downs or 3rd & long. But we have to be careful calling this play on 3rd down. It takes a long time to develop and may not be able to beat a typical 5- or 6-man, 3rd down blitz. If opponent study indicates that a blitz is not coming on 3rd down, then this is a great 3rd & long call. Otherwise, it is best to roll with this one on base downs.

## PRE-SNAP:

Florida's safeties show a pre-snap 2-high look, indicating either Cover 4 or Cover 2. The depth of the corners solidify the Cover 4 read as they are both playing 7-10 yards off the ball (Cover 2 corners will either be pressed or no more than 5 yards off). Furthermore, all of the DBs and linebackers are playing with zone eyes (eyes on the quarterback). If the defense is showing us more than one indication of a certain coverage, we should believe what they are telling us.

## POST-SNAP:

Florida's post-snap movement reveals true Cover 4 – a 4 deep, 3 underneath defense. The Gators rush just 4 against Alabama's 5, so protection is a non-issue. As #1 and #2 strong get into their deep over routes, the field corner and field safety must squeeze to those verticals since there are no other immediate threats entering their zones. The deep over by #2 weak hasn't even crossed the Mike linebacker at this point. By following those decoy routes, the field corner and field safety vacate that entire half of the field, and the deep over receiver walks into the end zone untouched.

The unsung hero of this play is actually the running back on the swing route. His route is what prohibits the field curl/flat defender from sinking underneath #2 weak and potentially taking away this throw. The field curl/flat defender is the main conflict defender because if he does sink, then we can throw the ball to the back in the flat and he'll have at least 15 yards of running room until he faces contact. But if that defender does not sink, and he holds the curl/flat zone, then we are going over the top for 6 every time. Obviously, we prefer the explosive touchdown, but it is important to teach our quarterbacks to take what the defense gives us and consistently make the correct decisions.

## ADJUSTMENTS:

The only base coverage that may give us fits on this play is Cover 3. Deep 1/3 corners must adhere to stricter zone guidelines than deep 1/4 defenders; and a disciplined corner is most likely staying home on this play. Even so, we can still hit #2 weak on the deep over if we adjust the depth of his route. Rather than work up-field after crossing the Mike linebacker, if the V angles towards the sideline, we will be able to hit him in the curl zone about 12 yards deep. This still puts the field curl/flat defender in conflict without running the deep over into the deep 1/3 corner.

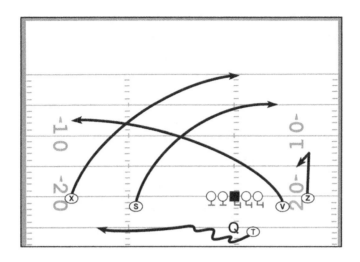

*Cross Country Adjustment — Cover 3 Beater*

# 25

## BOUNDARY FADE

### 2017 ACC CHAMPIONSHIP

### CLEMSON TIGERS VS. MIAMI HURRICANES

**— CHAMPION —**

**CLEMSON TIGERS**

# BOUNDARY FADE

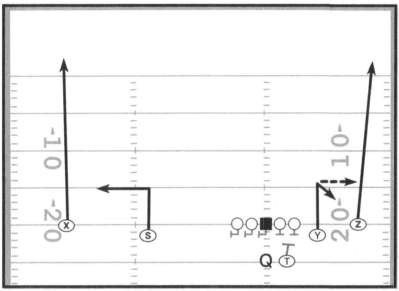

| POSITION | ALIGNMENT | ASSIGNMENT | COACHING NOTE |
|----------|-----------|------------|---------------|
| Q | GUN | DBP | 1ST READ - BOUNDARY FADE; 2ND READ - STICK |
| T | SPLIT OG/OT; 1 YD BEHIND QB | PASS PRO | PROTECT MAN SIDE |
| X | FIELD TOP #s | FADE | HOLD TOP #s UNTIL BALL TAKES YOU OFF |
| Z | BOUND. BOT. #s | FADE | FADE TO 5 YDS FROM SL UNTIL BALL IS THROWN; QB WILL TAKE YOU TO SL |
| S | FIELD HASH -2 | 5-YD OUT | SQUARE CUT |
| Y | DIV. EOL & Z | STICK | MAN COVERAGE = CONTINUE TO SIDELINE. ZONE COVERAGE = SIT IN OPEN ZONE |
| OL | BASE | 60 | PS = RT; 6-MAN PASS PRO; HALF SLIDE LT |

**FORMATION: GW DOUBLES**
**PERSONNEL: 11**
**MOTION: N/A**

## SCHEME:

Throwing a boundary fade in the red zone is a common and effective way to put your best receiver in a position to showcase his talents. The boundary fade is a much easier completion than the field fade because it requires a shorter throw. Not only does it beat man coverages like Cover 1 and Cover 0, it also has its place against common zone schemes like Cover 2, Cover 3, and Cover 4.

Since we are in the red zone and our space is limited, the goal does not need to be getting behind the defense. Rather, we are trying to position our receiver in the best spot to win a 1-on-1 matchup for us, whether that is an over-the-shoulder fade to the back pylon, a back shoulder fade to the front pylon, or even a jump ball.

## PRE-SNAP:

There's no pre-snap secret strategy to manipulate the defense on this play. This is a classic example of the my guy is better than your guy philosophy. Miami lines up pre-snap in exactly what they plan on running, 4-2-5 Cover 1 Hole. Each vertical threat is marked by a man coverage defender, the 2 backers are banjo-ing the back, and the post safety is sitting in the middle of the field.

Likewise, Clemson does not implement any pre-snap motions or irregular alignments; they just dare the Canes to stop them.

POST-SNAP:

This is a simple vert/out concept by Clemson – #1 runs a vertical, #2 runs an out. Miami brings a 4-man rush, which is no match for Clemson's 6-man protection. The quarterback has all day to throw and it's up to the receivers to beat their man 1-on-1.

The key to beating Cover 1 is to recognize the leverage with which the DBs are playing. Single-high safety coverages must obey the rules of the divider – an imaginary vertical line that dictates a DB's leverage. Dividers can be different for every team, but standard dividers are on the bottom of the numbers to the boundary, and halfway between the hash and the numbers to the field. If the ball is in the middle of the field, then both of the dividers are on the top of the numbers.

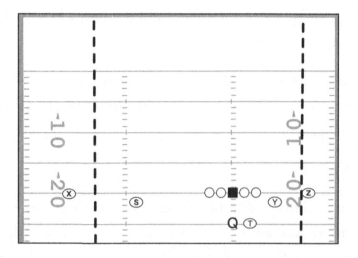

*Dividers When the Ball Is on the Hash*

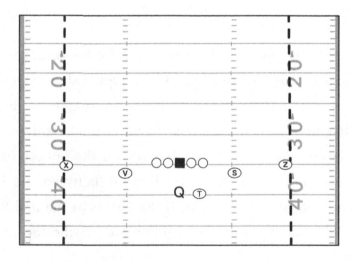

*Dividers When the Ball is in the Middle of the Field*

If a receiver to the boundary is lined up outside of the bottom of the numbers, he is outside the divider. Similarly, if he is lined up inside the bottom of the numbers, then he is inside the divider. The same concept applies to the field divider.

When a receiver is lined up outside of the divider, then the corner will align with inside leverage and play the receiver 1-on-1. He cannot count on post safety help; his only help is the sideline. If the receiver is lined up inside the divider, then the corner will align with outside leverage. He will still play the receiver man-to-man, but with the intention of funneling him towards his middle of the field help, the post safety.

As a receiver, it is not necessary to learn where the dividers are for each team you play because the leverage of the DB will tell you. They are always going to play the leverage opposite of their help. So, if the DB is outside of you, you are inside the divider, and he is counting on his middle of the field help. If the DB is inside of you, then you are outside the divider and his only help is the sideline.

So, how does this knowledge help us beat Cover 1? We need to attack the DB's leverage because once he loses his leverage, he loses his help.

Clemson's Z receiver executes this concept perfectly. His corner is playing him outside leverage, so he knows he needs to eventually win to the outside. As the ball is snapped, he stems towards the inside shoulder of the corner, causing him to shuffle inside. As the corner is shuffling inside, the Z sticks his foot in the ground, cuts back to the outside and overtakes the corner's leverage. This puts the defense in a bind because the man defender and the help defender are now both on the inside of the receiver; there is no outside leverage defender.

The receiver is now in a true 1-on-1 situation with the corner because the safety cannot cover the ground necessary to help on the outside of the divider. The quarterback delivers a well-thrown fade ball down the boundary sideline and hits his receiver in stride for the touchdown.

## ADJUSTMENTS:

It is important to note that due to the considerable amount of action seen in the boundary, defenses will often travel their best corner into the boundary on every down. This may or may not change how we feel about the boundary fade matchup. We may need to swap our X and Z receivers in order to tip the scale back in our favor. Either way, we must be aware of the matchup we are getting before blindly throwing the ball up in the end zone – turnovers down there are costly.

# CONCLUSION

---

*"The only yardstick for success our society has is being a champion."*

— COACH JOHN MADDEN

---

EACH ONE OF the offensive concepts that we have studied throughout this playbook is proven to produce positive results in the biggest moments. Whether we need a long-bomb touchdown or a critical 3$^{rd}$ & short conversion, these 25 plays have us covered. They feature an extremely wide variety of ways in which we can attack the defense, including: base gap and zone run schemes; misdirections; read options; run pass options; play action passes; short, intermediate, and deep drop back pass concepts; quick game; double moves; and 1-on-1 mismatch exploitations. If you need a championship-winning play, *Touchdown Genius* has it.

Stay tuned for the remaining books in this series, as we will expand both the breadth and depth of our championship-level knowledge. As much analysis as was covered in this book, we have only begun to scratch the surface.

XOS Playmaking exists to serve you. The goal is to maximize your football potential, regardless of the degree at which you participate, be it a coach, player, or fan. Feel free to leave a review and provide honest feedback regarding the manner in which this content served you, as well as additional content you wish to see broken down in future publications.

In the meantime, get out there and install these 25 plays to your newfound, championship-winning playbook.

Made in the USA
Las Vegas, NV
20 December 2023

83285794R00154